Blendon

from the earliest times

by Roger Mayo

This book is dedicated to my parents Owen and Lorna, and my sister, Shirley, who first took me to Blendon in the 1950s.

No part of this publication may be reproduced, stored in a retrieval system, or transmitted in any form or by any means, electronic, mechanical, photocopying, recording or otherwise without prior permission of the publisher.

© 2002 Bexley Council
Directorate of Education and Leisure Services
Roger Mayo

ISBN No. 0902541609

Cover photo: Aerial photo of Blendon Hall, c.1925

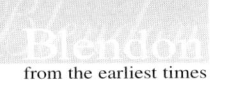

Acknowledgements

I would like to express my gratitude to all the people who have contributed to the project. Apart from Jim Bowyer and Geoff Holland without whom this would never have happened, special thanks go to Stuart Bligh, Oliver Wooller, Frances Sweeny, Sue Barclay and all the team at the Local Studies and Archive Centre for their patience, detailed guidance and proofing, Jessica Vale, Museum Collections Manager at Bexley Museum and particularly Jim Packer, local historian who has been so helpful and Rod le Gear.

I would also like to thank Iris Brooker and Ray Jeal for their tireless research, help and constant 'digging', Richard Lea and Treve Rosoman from English Heritage, Carolynn Boucher for her genealogical research, Roy Hopper, Ron Anthony, Bill Neale, Marion Smith and all the residents of the estate, especially Pat and David Taylor, Mike and Heather Caley and Mr and Mrs Dave Close, Ray and Ruth Smith, The Reverend Alan Keeler and Barry Mathews.

A special mention to all those who were related to people who worked on the Estate without whom Chapter 10 would not have been possible – especially Miss Hazel Hall, Mr and Mrs Johnson and their grandson Ian, Mr and Mrs Cottrell, the late Mrs Bene (Elsie) Reddall nee Beckenham and Mike and Margaret Clinch.

For his patience on the design and layout of this book my thanks to John Hunter and also to Gary Fairman and the Graphics Team at Bexley Council. Thank you also to Les Chester for his detailed indexing.

The illustration acknowledgements appear at the back of the book but I would particularly like to thank Paul Linnington (artist) who created the painting of Blendon, which forms the cover of the book.

Finally, I would like to thank my wife Stella for all her support, help and patience – without which I could not have undertaken this venture.

Roger Mayo

Woking, Surrey 2002

from the earliest times

Contents

		Page
Acknowledgements		*Opposite*
Aerial Photograph of the Hall		4
Preface		5
Chapter 1	Introduction	9
Chapter 2	Murder most foul – and earliest references to 1730	13
Chapter 3	Heroes and Villains – the early eighteenth century	23
Chapter 4	Love's Labours Lost – the 1730s	35
Chapter 5	The end of the Sawbridge connection and the building of the new hall – 1763–1807	47
Chapter 6	The Smiths – Part 1 – Bankers and Builders 'Tenax in Fide' – 1807–1824	55
Chapter 7	Between the Smiths – The Campbells – 1825–1839	69
Chapter 8	Oswald Smith – Bankers and Builders – Part II The Heyday of the Hall – 1839–1863	83
Chapter 9	The Americans are coming! William Cunliffe Pickersgill – and Anna Riggs Jay – 1863–1929	93
Chapter 10	The Staff at Blendon	117
Chapter 11	Decline, Fall and Transformation "Enter the Guvnor"	127
Postscript – Reflections		139
Appendix I	James Pattison in New York – 1779–1780	143
Appendix II	Garden Life Article – 1903	149
Appendix III	Wedding Report Rodwell-Jay – 1910	152
Illustration Acknowledgements		154
Places to Go		154
Footnotes		156
Index		160

Brendon
from the earliest times

Fig 1. Aerial photo of Hall c1925. In the background are two horses, Tom and Warrior

Preface

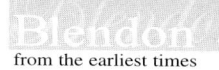

In this preface I want to explain briefly why we started the 'Blendon Project' and also explain the background to what we know today.

There are three reasons why I have become involved in this project.

Firstly, as a child living locally, Blendon intrigued me. In the sixties you could peer through the railings in The Avenue at the half drained lake. You could stand and wonder at the incongruous Jay's Cottages (with the cottage doors so obviously designed for children to knock on) and then walk on to the old lodge at the end of Blendon Parade. You could then cross Blendon Road (relatively easily!) and look at, and touch, the old horse trough that stood outside The Three Blackbirds.

Fig 2. Blendon Road from Blackfen showing The Three Blackbirds, horse trough and Jay's Cottages in background in the 1950s. (Bexley Local Studies)

Preface

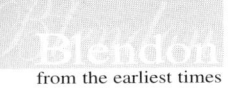

All these artefacts were out of place and out of time – crying out to the curious. Our home, a bungalow in The Sanctuary, had its mysteries; a power cable running vertically down a skirting board, feeding power to somewhere inaccessible below the building; strange noises and the odd smell that we could not trace. Next door, our neighbours' garden had steps descending into a cellar or shelter from which you could go through and emerge into another garden in Beechway. Then in 1994 whilst on business in Bexley I was able to visit Bexley Local Studies at Hall Place and discovered that our old home in The Sanctuary appeared to 'sit' completely within the walls of the old Hall.

The second reason for the project is that there *is* a story to tell about Blendon. We want to share this with residents – both present and past – and others who may be interested. It is a story that has not yet been told. There is no specific text written on the area. There are fact sheets, which give some tantalising titbits, some research and people's memories.[1,2] Chief amongst those who remember Blendon as it was, must be Jim Bowyer. He is the son of D C Bowyer, who bought the whole eighty-eight acre estate and Hall in 1929 for £29,000 from the trustees of the late W C Pickersgill. Jim, whom I first met in 1998, is a rich source of information on Blendon. Jim himself worked in the Lodge on Blendon Road from 1931 until his retirement in 1985. His memory and recollection of events is first-class. He has been a constant source of encouragement and enthusiasm to me.

The third reason for the project, and one that has sustained my interest since the end of 1999, is the tremendous interest shown by residents – both past and present – in the history of the Estate.

In December 1999, I leaflet-dropped properties in Beechway and The Sanctuary together with the few properties that are still standing that were contemporary to the Hall. It was through this initial 'letter drop' that I met Geoff Holland who lives in the last house to be built under Jim Bowyer's auspices. Geoff has always had a keen interest in Blendon and we have worked together on the project since meeting. His own garden had proved a treasure trove of interest. (It is located within an area of the estate referred to, appropriately, as the 'Pleasure Grounds' at the head of the top lake.) Geoff has always kindly given me time and help – and a lot of hospitality.

The winter and spring of 2000 were spent speaking with local residents, exploring and explaining unusual garden features. We also examined and passed on artefacts to Jessica Vale, Museum Collections Manager at Bexley Museum for dating and assessment.

Preface

Fig 3. Southerly view of the Hall across the lake dating from early 20th century and taken from the area which is now north of The Drive and west of The Avenue. Some yuccas survive round what was the old lake. On the southerly side of the Hall is the single storey conservatory. To the right, steps lead up to the French windows into the Library. (Bexley Local Studies)

In early July we gave the first talk on the Blendon Hall Estate at St. James the Great in Blendon.[3] It was appropriate to discuss the estate at one of its spiritual homes. The estate was leaflet-dropped and over 250 people packed into the Hall on a warm summer's evening to hear the talk. As a result and a consequent article in the News Shopper[4], much of the autumn of 2000 was spent processing all the material, artefacts and lines of enquiry that arose. During 2001 two further public talks were held – both events selling out to over 150 people each.[5,6]

We are slowly unravelling the Blendon story: Jim Bowyer, Geoff Holland and myself, ably assisted by experts in their respective fields of archaeology, local history and genealogy.

What we could never have predicted was the variety of material that has been presented to us over the two years of active research. Items have ranged from a medieval spoon that has been forwarded to the British Museum for

Preface

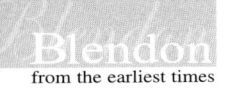

investigation, coins, pieces of Blendon Hall chimney pots; old plates used at the Hall, a cartwheel spanner – and even an original flagpole which, as you will discover in the book, may well have had the Stars and Stripes flying at its head!

The documentary evidence, as you will read, has been just as varied; ranging from correspondence from the Hall in the early nineteenth century to works of famous people in which Blendon prominently features through to detailed inventories that tell us much about the whole estate. Postcards of the Hall from the early twentieth century have also thrown a great deal of light on day-to-day issues.

Much of the documentary evidence has been easily accessible but some has called for determined hunting and specialist help in deciphering. I think it is fair to say that we have had some very good fortune in our enquiries.

It does not end here. The research will continue beyond the publication of this book, as will the talks. I am sure we will discover more that will add to our knowledge.

Fig 4. Bottom Lake and grounds from inside the Hall. The pathway follows the course of The Avenue today. The iron hurdle fencing separating the fields is visible. This fencing parallels today's Beechway. The sweet chestnut trees in the centre of the photo still stand. (Bexley Local Studies)

Chapter One

Introduction

The purpose of this book is to share with the reader the history of Blendon. Blendon is located in the Borough of Bexley, west of Bexley Village and south of Bexleyheath. The estate is approximately 11 miles south-east from London Bridge on the border of Kent and Greater London. This book aims to take the story from earliest times to the present day, in particular, the findings of the "Blendon Project" that has been conducted over the past two years.

Our knowledge is constantly being added to – this book is a 'living' document. – a record of what we know, and believe, to date. It is set in the context of the ongoing Blendon Project research and talks.

The structure of the book is in the form of a timeline. It covers Roman times to the present day. Our knowledge of the recent past is far more detailed than of earlier times – but there are some tantalising glimpses of earlier periods. We have tried to integrate finds and artefacts in their appropriate time periods – although this is not always easy. There are footnotes for references to other texts and papers, if the reader wishes to explore these further. In the Appendix there are some detailed extracts.

The style of the book is non-technical and conversational. It is intended as a stimulating and enjoyable read – rather than as an academic tome. I hope you feel the enthusiasm that has kept us going.

The Hall and the Estate – the basic facts

When Blendon Hall estate was put up for sale at auction on 26 November 1863, it was described as comprising:

> "A First-Class Mansion affording ample accommodation for a family of distinction, most delightfully situate on a gravelly soil in a finely-timbered park of about 85 acres adorned with an ornamental sheet of water beautifully laid out pleasure grounds, avenues and walks."[7]

It sold for £24,000 to Mr W C Pickersgill of New York. When the estate was sold again by direction of the trustees of Mr W C Pickersgill's estate, it was described as "about 88 acres".[8]

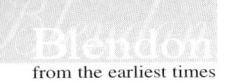

Introduction

Fig 5. The Three Black Birds at Blendon on the north of the Estate. There has been a licensed public house here since at least 1717. The freehold was intermittently in the hands of the owners of Blendon Hall. It is said that senior staff at the Hall would send out for a bottle of drink from the pub. (Bexley Local Studies)

Therefore for the purposes of this book, we are defining the Blendon Estate as a parcel of land bordered on the west by Penhill Road, on the north by Blendon Road (with some excursions into land further north), on the east by Elmwood Drive (formerly Tanyard Lane) and on the south by the River Shuttle. The Ordnance Survey references for the four 'corners' of this land are as follows; Penhill Road /River Shuttle (south west corner) 547272,173473; Penhill Road / Blendon Road (north west corner) 547352,174204; Bridgen Road/ Elmwood Drive (north east corner) 548148,174038; Elmwood Drive/ River Shuttle (south east corner) 548105,173767. [9]

The land is set on two distinct plateaux falling from 118 feet to 66 feet in a general northwest to east/southeast direction. The main feature on the estate was the Hall – a building dating from 1763 of brick and stucco construction. It is on the site of a former, much earlier building.

The Hall that was demolished in 1934 was a large country 'villa', often used by its owners and tenants as a country seat to which they would 'retire' from their London home. (See Repton's description of the Hall in Chapter 6.)

Introduction

The Hall was described in the Kentish Times of 28th June 1929 as comprising the following:

> "The old-world mansion contains hall, dining–room, drawing-room, study, billiard room, music room, library, conservatory, 14 principal bed and dressing-rooms, 2 bathrooms, 8 servants' bedrooms, and 3 attic bedrooms and complete domestic offices. Garages and stabling. Matured gardens and grounds, including an ornamental lake of almost 2 acres. A set of good farm buildings. Lodges, cottages, bailiff's house and in addition well timbered parkland."[10]

The owners and tenants of the estate were mainly 'distinguished' families – some heroes, some villains – often titled, with mercantile or military connections. Some were MPs or JPs. They did not derive their living from the estate – they were usually well established before moving in. The domestics were drawn from local families and often interrelated – on the basis that when a position arose it was safer to choose someone from an existing employee's family.

A brief timeline shows the major events in the life of the Estate. These are described in the following chapters in more detail.

Fig 6. Skaters on the Lake, probably in the 1920s (Bexley Local Studies)

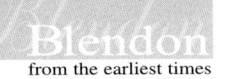

Introduction

Blendon Timeline

13c First written references to 'Bladindon'
1241 Roger of Bladindon was surety to Roger of Blackwenne at Canterbury Assize
1283 John of Bladindon, Reeve of Bexley
1301 Agnes of Bladindon's goods described in Subsidy Rolls
1400 Henry of Castelayn Keeper of the Archbishop's Forests lives at Blendon.
1608 Manorial Survey
1620s The Derings of Pluckley at Blendon
1640s The Wroth family – Royalists at Blendon
1672 Sir Edward Brett – Royalist hero – lives at Blendon
1681 Manorial Survey details the estate
1684 Brett Fisher – linked with Lamorbey and father in law of Jacob Sawbridge – Director of South Sea Trading Company
1730's Wesleys & Whitefield preach regularly at Blendon, Bexley & Blackheath.
1760's Lady Mary Scott builds her 'neat mansion'
1783 General James Pattison RA buys Blendon
1807 John Smith banker and MP buys Blendon
1811 3 Roman urns found on estate containing human remains
1816 Gothic alterations under architect John Shaw and Repton's landscaping
1824 William and Anna Maria Campbell buy Blendon
1830's Letters from Fanny Campbell & Harriet Lambert. Listings of fixtures/ fittings
1840 Oswald Smith, nephew of John Smith, buys Blendon
1853 Wedding of Oswald Smith's daughter Frances to Claude Bowes Lyon
1854 Cricket match between Blendon Hall and West Kent Cricket Club
1863 WC Pickersgill, an American banker, buys estate on Oswald Smith's death
1891 Pickersgill dies. Mr Carl Jay & Mrs Anna Jay (Pickersgill's daughter) move to Blendon
1900 Major Phipps Hornby wins VC at Sanna's Post in Boer War
1905 Written record of domestic service at Hall
1919 Warrior the horse, who towed the gun carriage for the Unknown Warrior, retires to Blendon
1925 Celebration of four generations of Jays at Hall
1929 Death of Mrs Jay. Sale of estate to D.C. Bowyer. House items & farm equipment auctioned.
1934 Demolition of Hall & sale of fixtures and fittings
1931–1936 Building of modern estate
1940's Destruction of houses in Bladindon Drive in WWII
1980's Draining of lower lake and building of houses

Fig 7. Blendon Timeline. This shows a number of significant events in the history of the Estate.

Chapter Two

Murder most foul – and earliest references to 1730

In the Rev. F de P Castell's book on "Bexleyheath & Welling" (1910) he refers to:

> "In 1811 three Roman urns with human remains were found on the Blendon Hall Estate"[11]

The Woolwich Antiquarian Society Volume 14 in 1931 refers to:

> "Blendon Hall – Three urns and a broken one with bones found in 1811"

This document also refers to the finding of a Roman coin.[12]

Bladinton, Bladynton and Bladigdon all come from the Old English, which means:

> "the farm of the people who live by the dark water"

In the thirteenth century there is a reference to Bladindon Court. Henry and Eadwin of Bladindon were prominent tenants of Bexley Manor. In Du Boulay's Medieval Bexley (first edition) Henry of Blendon is in a yoke in 1210 (a yoke was about 40 acres of land) and Henry would have paid some sort of rental for the right to work the land.[13] Robert of Bladindon in 1241 served on the jury of the Canterbury assizes (this suggests that Robert was rich enough to own a horse and that he had at least one serf who could take care of his cattle whilst he was away from home).[14] In that same assize Roger of Bladindon was surety to Roger of Blackwenne in Bixle who slew John de la Welle and fled. There's nothing like a medieval murder to start a story – we know who dunnit – but we do not know why he dunnit – or what poor Roger of Bladindon had to pay or forfeit because Roger of Blackwenne had 'done a runner'.[15]

In 1283 John of Bladindon, Reeve of Bexley (the bailiff or steward) earned a one off payment of 5 shillings (25p) for organising the tenants on the 250 acres of demesne land. At the appropriate season he ensured that the ploughing, sowing, hoeing, reaping and threshing were done. He allotted the work of keeping the mills in working order, re-thatching the barns and repairing the fences. He also ensured that each group of tenants carted eight cartloads of hay and eight cartloads of fuel to the barns of the Manor House behind St Mary's Church. The

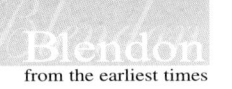

Murder most foul – and earliest references to 1730

reeveship was no sinecure but John of Blendon had his compensations for his work as reeve. He held more land that anyone else in the manor. He received a stipend of five shillings a year and had an allowance of wheat. Besides these material rewards he was the recognised leader of the tenants and he would meet, if not the archbishop himself, at least his representative when the accounts were presented.[16] In a list of twenty yokes of land in Bexley in 1283/4 the sixth yoke was shared between this John of Bladindon and Stephen at Halle. John had all his 33 acres together in this one yoke.[17] The seventh yoke was shared between Ralph de Bladyndon and six others.

W Mandy in the Woolwich and District Antiquarian Society article on 'Collections for the Early History of Bexley and Dartford' in 1915 notes that Agnes, probably John's widow, paid the highest tax in Bexley. In 1301 her goods are described in the Subsidy Rolls. The Subsidy Rolls were a device to exact a tax equivalent to one fifteenth of the value of one's goods. Agnes's goods are listed as follows:

> One horse (equus), 2 hacks, 2 bullocks, 2 steers, 7 cows, 4 calves, 8 pigs, 12 porkers, 20 sheep, 1 lead cistern, loose cash - 6s 8d Total: £18 10s 0d of which a fifteenth is stated as 9s 1d.

This is mathematically incorrect. The total amount levied is a fortieth of her value – it should be £1 4s 8d. Alternatively fifteen times 9 shillings and a penny is £6 16s 3d.[18]

A subsequent John of Bladindon was a lawyer. He and his wife Maud were wealthy and influential people in the area (c1325). A beautiful monumental brass (see illustration) commemorating them is preserved in St Michael's Church in East Wickham. It is described thus at the end of the nineteenth century.

"In 1887, the ancient brass was restored by a subscription. The brass consists of two half-length figures, male and female, within a handsome floriated cross, on the long shaft of which remains part of the inscription, in Norman French: "Johan de

Fig 8. Monumental brass of John and Maud of Bladindon in St Michael's Church in East Wickham.

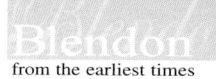

Murder most foul – and earliest references to 1730

Bladigdone et Maud sa feme." The word "feme", being missing, had to be supplied. The continuation of the inscription, together with half the shaft and base of the cross, have long disappeared. The brass is very old; the date is probably 1325, and it is believed to be the oldest example extant of a male figure clad in civil costume. At some time since 1809, the brass became detached from the stone and was placed in the drawer of a table in the vestry. When, subsequently, the church was broken into by thieves, the cross was used by the burglars to prise open a cupboard, and was thus broken into several pieces, all of which were found and preserved…Johan de Bladigdone (or Blendon) is believed to have rebuilt the church, the architecture of which is about his assumed date." [19] It is believed that these people would have been wealthy enough to live in a timber framed hall house similar to the one that was located in North Cray Road. This has been restored to its original condition and can now be seen at the Weald & Downland Museum at Singleton, near Chichester in West Sussex.[20]

Fig 9. Timber framed hall house at the Weald & Downland Museum at Singleton, near Chichester in West Sussex (Reproduced by kind permission of Weald and Downland Open Air Museum, Singleton, Chichester, West Sussex)

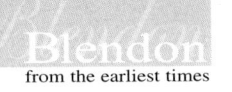

Murder most foul – and earliest references to 1730

In 1377 Jordan of Bladindon (possibly the grandson of John and Maud above) transferred the Hall and Estate to the Walsinghams.[21] From 1381 – 1407, Henry Castelayn of Bexley, Keeper of the Archbishop's Forests, held Blendon on cornage or horn tenure. Henry paid the Archbishop rent based on the number of head of cattle raised on the land. According to a pay roll of the time he earned £10 a year, got free fuel and one suit with the Archbishop's badge on it.

In 1407 Henry died. He made his will on 4th April 1407 and must have died within a few days as probate of the will was granted to Simon Castilayn, his brother, William Cave and John Wynterfloed on the 19th of that month. Henry's will in the Register of the Archbishop of Canterbury, Thomas Arundel, survives at Lambeth Palace Library and a copy exists at Bexley Local Studies.[22] He directed that a chaplain should daily say mass for repose of his soul for two years.[23] Henry bequeathed six torches to the churches of Bexley, Earde (Crayford) and Eynsford and money for masses at the churches of Bexley and Crayford. Henry left his bees to St Mary's Church to supply wax for candles before the Image of the Virgin in the chancel and the Images of St Katherine and St Margaret. He also provided for a perpetual observance of the anniversary of his death, including 4d. for beer, 1d. for bread to the poor, 2d. for each parish clerk, 2d for the bell ringer and 3d. for oblation annually at the altar.[24] Henry also provided £2 for a new west window (the stonework is in the decorated style of the time). He gave 20 shillings (one pound) for the repair of two roads leading from Blendon towards the royal palaces of Eltham and Greenwich. Perhaps he had suffered from the ruts and mire on his way to the royal palaces of Greenwich and Eltham. One of these roads was called Blakeben or Blakeven Strete that led from Bladyndon to the Blakeben Gate or Blakeven Gate of the Danson Estate. (Blakeben is now Blackfen.)

The Horn Brass on the north wall of the north aisle of St Mary's Church, Bexley, commemorates Henry. It is a

Fig 10. Horn Brass - Henry Castelayn (Bexley Local Studies)

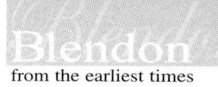

Murder most foul – and earliest references to 1730

hunting horn brass from which unfortunately two escutcheons and the inscription have been missing for centuries. It is located near the Champneis memorial and is thought to be unique.[25]

Hasted states that towards the end of Henry IV's reign (about 1410) the estate was sold to Ferbie of St Paul's Cray-Hill. One of his descendants in the 1420's passed the Estate to William Marshall who transferred it not long afterwards to Rawlins. Rawlins, and subsequently his son, actually lived at the Hall but there is no evidence to suggest that his successor, Nathaniel May did.[26]

There is an unattributed reference to the fact that William Camden, the noted antiquary, lived at Blendon in the sixteenth century.

By 1608, Thomas Wroth held the Blendon estate for Peter, his nephew and we have a manorial survey for Bexley extant from that date. It details the free tenants, occupiers, name and description of property, state of cultivation and extent. Thomas Wroath (sic) is listed as a free tenant (i.e. the person claiming to hold the property) 'by charter of Nathaniel Maye, formerly said N Maye's or Richard Beckingham's – Rent 48s 10d'. There are a number of occupiers listed with varying amounts of land and types of properties. Whilst it is not possible to identify Blendon Hall directly, the most probable candidate is the property and land occupied by Anne Sherley, (the widowed sister in law of Wroth)[27] and others. In total the property covers 73 acres and is a mix of arable, meadow, pasture and marsh. The messuage (dwelling) barn etc., orchard and garden are described as occupying just over an acre. Names for the areas listed include; Stone, Claper, le Bottom, le Mead before the gate, le Crofte, Good Luck Field, Long Field, le Lodge, Puck's Field, 2 closes, Dewlandes, North Field, Pollises Mead.[28]

When Peter Wroth died in May 1644, he charged his brother Sir Thomas Wroth to pay £10 as a stock for the benefit of the poor of Bexley.[29] John, Peter's eldest son, was fighting as a Royalist for Charles I in the Civil War. John had married Ann, daughter of Toby, Lord Caulfield, and widow of Sir Paul Harris.[30] John fought with distinction at the battle of Newbury. During the Commonwealth (1649 – 1660), following the execution of Charles I, Royalists were forced to pay compounding fines – in effect fines for fighting 'on the wrong side'. Consequently, John Wroth had to mortgage the estate and his lands in Plumstead and Woolwich for 1000 years in order to pay the fines. He mortgaged the estate to Francis Hill, a lawyer, of Lincolns Inn. On Cromwell's death, Wroth became a Commissioner of the Militia. Following the Restoration, in 1660, John Wroth was created a baronet. He died in 1671 and

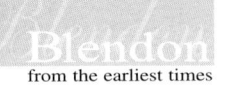

Murder most foul – and earliest references to 1730

Wroth of Blendon Hall

Baronetage created 29th November 1660

Extinct 27th June 1722

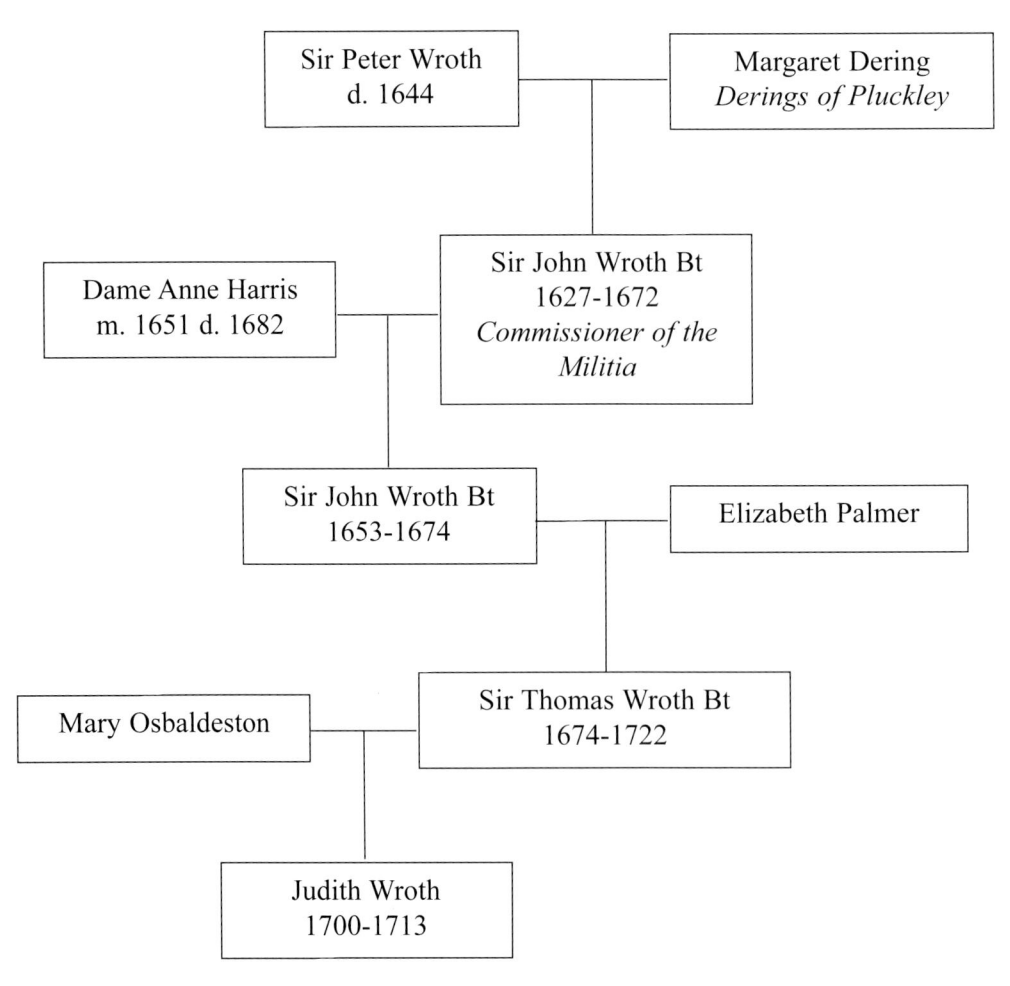

```
        Sir Peter Wroth ─────── Margaret Dering
           d. 1644                Derings of Pluckley
                 │
Dame Anne Harris ─── Sir John Wroth Bt
m. 1651 d. 1682         1627-1672
                     Commissioner of the
                          Militia
                 │
            Sir John Wroth Bt ─── Elizabeth Palmer
               1653-1674
                 │
Mary Osbaldeston ─── Sir Thomas Wroth Bt
                        1674-1722
                 │
            Judith Wroth
              1700-1713
```

Fig 11. The Wroth Family Tree and Crest. This branch of the Wroth family were nearly all Royalists but 'were not wholly uncritical of the King' (Ruth Hutcherson) *Sources: Burkes Extinct Baronetcies 1844. The Complete Baronetage - George Edward Cokayne*

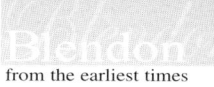

Murder most foul – and earliest references to 1730

the estate passed to his son and heir, Sir John Wroth, subject to the mortgage term granted by his father.[31]

When his son, Thomas, died in 1722 the baronetcy became extinct.[32]

In 1672, Edward Brewster took over responsibility for the loan and took possession of the Estate. The Estate became the home of Sir Edward Brett.[33] Sir Edward had served under Gustavus Adolphus, the King of Sweden, in Germany and then was called upon by King Charles to assist him in the English Civil War. Early in the war Captain Brett is listed in the muster roll in an expedition under the Earl of Northumberland after the army's retreat from Newcastle into Yorkshire.[34] He is then listed in the King's Lifeguard of Horse, which was raised in 1642 and served in the war in attendance upon the King. The regiment was made up of two troops and in 1644 Major (Sir) Edward Brett led a troop of the Queen's Regiment.[35] In this year the troop accompanied the Queen to Exeter. During this time Brett received the honour of knighthood from the King's hands in open field on horseback – at Lostwithiel for suppressing the rebels in Cornwall.

Colonel Sir Edward Brett is then listed in the Royal Regiment of Horse (Guards) at its first muster on 16th February 1661. He is captain of his own troop with Henry Slingsby listed as cornet (see beneficiaries of will below). Slingsby was the second son of the royalist Sir Henry Slingsby who was beheaded by Cromwell in 1658.[36] In 1664 Brett was commissioned to lead companies to York to 'rescue the country from the dangerous attempts of seditious conventicles' (the Conventicle Act came into force in July 1664).[37]

Latterly Brett served in the Netherlands in the service of the Prince of Orange and continued in his command for several years after the restoration. He is also listed as a commissioner or collector for disbanding the regiments in 1677 for Middlesex and Westminster City.[38] In his later years he could ride from Blendon to London to fulfil his duties as the Sergeant Porter to the King's Majesty and to meet his friends - including Samuel Pepys.[39]

In 1681 a Manorial Survey was carried out in which Brett's, and others' properties at Blendon are described over three pages in copperplate handwriting and the total value on which Blendon is assessed is £168. This formed the basis for rental to be paid to the Lord of the Manor – Oxford University. About this time Lady Mary Gerard-Cosein was, for a few years, a tenant at the Hall. She was originally Lady Mary Berkeley who married Sir Gilbert Gerrard but was divorced in 1684 within a short time of her wedding. She died in 1693 at the age of 28.[40] There is a marble memorial to her over the south door at St Mary's,

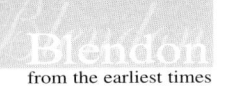

Murder most foul – and earliest references to 1730

Bexley. She was the daughter of Sir Charles Berkeley, Keeper of the Privy Purse to King Charles II who in 1664 created him Earl of Falmouth. The Earl was killed in action at sea against the Dutch on 3rd June 1665 on board the 'Royal Charles'. [41]

Brett ended his days at Blendon Hall, dying in 1684 aged 75 and is buried in the grounds of Bexley church. His will illustrates his colourful life:

'PROBATE of Will dated 22 December 1682 with Codicil dated 7 November 1683 of Sir Edward Brett, of Blendenhall, parish of Bexley, Co. Kent, kt., and Serjeant Porter to the King's Majesty. Recites his purchase of Blendon Hall from Brewster, and states that he had never been able to acquire the 1000 year term of 16 February 1657/8 because Sir John Wroth was dead and his heir only 8 years old. Desires that a conveyance be executed when the Wroth heirs are of age…Lists tenants {of testator} as Lock, Crowcher, Nunn, Harris, Bancks, Watts, Small, Bexley, Rich and Parry. Bequeathes the property to the sons of Henry Fisher, of Greeton, C. North., gent., in tail male, naming John, Nathaniel, and Edward, such persons to take the name Brett. Grants an annuity of £40 to Elizabeth, wife of said Henry Fisher, and one of £20 to Richard Watson. Bequeathes to the children of his niece, Anne Isham, the daughter of his sister, Mary Isham, viz., Richard Wathew, John Wathew, Henry Wathew, Alice Wathew, and Sarah Wathew £500 to be divided amongst them; and £200 to the two daughters of his nephew Henry Isham late of Virginia, deceased, by Katherine his wife; and £400 to said John, Nathaniel and Edward Fisher; £50 to Alice Grove, of London, widow; £50 to his god daughter, Anne Grove; and £50 to his kinsman, Owen Norton; £50 to Captain Henry Slingsby, captain of a troop of horse in the Royal Regiment; £100 to Mrs. Margaret Browne; and £10 to John Martin, who was orderly man to testator's troop. Gives £100 to executors, Stephen Beckingham of Grayes Inn, esq., and Richard Watson, of St. Margaret's, Westminster, Co. Middlesex, gent.; £20 each to his servants, Agnis Harris and James Crafts; £10 each to god-children, the child of Emanuel Thomas and the son of Mrs. Brunce Clenth. Gives his "carpentine cup" to his cousin Charles Brett's widow, his "old cup with the Bretts armes thereupon engraven and tipt with silver" to his cousin Margaret Duncombe, widow. Gives to Mary Brett, widow of his late cousin Charles Brett, £200 together with his great cabinet and the china standing on it. Appoints £300 for his funeral and a monument. Bequeathes residue of real and personal estate to said John, Nathaniel and Edward Fisher.'

'[Notes in margin thus: The three Fishers died without issue; "Mr. Sawbridge is assignee, devisee, and executor of said John Brett Fisher; "John Brett Fisher was also heir at law of Sir Edward Brett and devised this estate and all other his real and personal estates to Mr. Sawbridge"; "Mr. Sawbridge's eldest son is heir at law of said John Brett Fisher, being grandson of Brett F's uncle"]

Witnesses: Elizabeth Rowse, Charles Edwards, Jane Jones, William Allam, scrivener.'

'Codicil desires his pictures to be taken to Blendenhall to be then kept with his other goods until John Fisher comes of age; Henry Fisher and his wife to have Blendenhall with its gardens and orchard rent-free until then. Gives £20 to Robert Norton.

Witnesses: Ann Loton, Elizabeth Rowse, William Allam, scrivener.'[42]

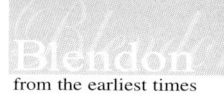

Murder most foul – and earliest references to 1730

Brett was clearly a very wealthy man and able to reward those close to him well.

Brett passed the estate to John Brett Fisher, his nephew's son. John Brett Fisher was a wealthy man and he lived there after Lady Mary Gerard – Cosein's death.[43] He married Judith Bourne who had inherited nearby Lamorbey with its considerable debts and obligations. With Brett Fisher's help the fortunes of the Lamorbey estate were restored and by 1700 the Bourne family was once again in possession of the Estate.[44] However, the Brett Fishers continued to reside at Blendon. In 1724 they sold Lamorbey to William Steele, a Director of the East India Company for £2,000.[45] Brett Fisher bought out John Wroth's interests in the estate in 1731. John Brett Fisher continued to live at Blendon and resided there until he died in 1732.

Apart from the documentary references and memorials in East Wickham and St Mary's Church what else comes down to us from this early period in Blendon's history?

There is a copper alloy spoon, which dates from this period. It is one of the most fascinating finds of the whole project. A resident of the estate found the spoon many years ago whilst working in his garden.

Jessica Vale, the Museum Collections Manager at Bexley Museum said: 'this is a very rare and unusual object. In its day it would have been a prestige item. There are references to spoons as bequests in wills.'[46]

The British Museum was not very sure about the item but believe it could date from the 15th to 17th century. They suggested it was of German manufacture. However, Bill Brown, a cutlery historian and author suggested an earlier date for the object – mid medieval (14th century) and thought it might come from the Netherlands. He also stated that spoons were often found in old compost heaps – being lost when scraping food plates.[47]

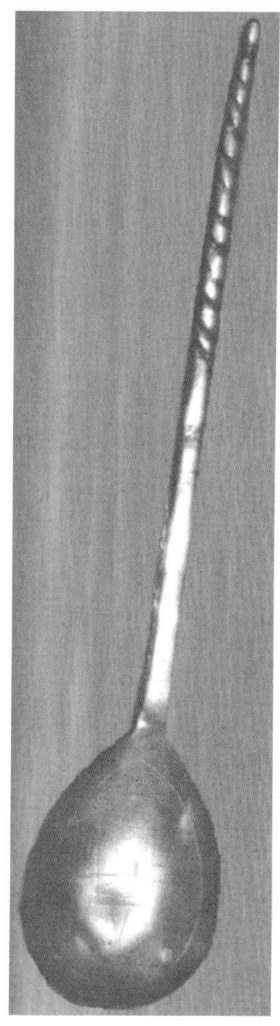

Fig 12. Brass Spoon. The bowl has a crude engraving of a religious building on it.

If the spoon had been found in its original setting – for example an old cesspit with other contemporary items then dating may have been easier.

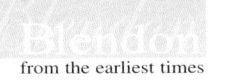

Murder most foul – and earliest references to 1730

Did Sir Edward Brett pick this item up whilst fighting as a young man in Germany or perhaps many years later the Low Countries? We will probably never know.

The finial (the tip or end of the spoon handle) is in an acorn derivative style. The stem is part twisted (top left to bottom right), squarish section. Perhaps most intriguing is the spoon – it is irregular pear-shaped – the back bearing a simple engraved design of a building with a central steeple.[48]

The dimensions of the spoon are as follows:

Length 135 mm, width of bowl 27 mm.

Apart from the spoon there is an old mulberry tree in The Sanctuary, which is said to date from Tudor times. There are some fragments of drains extant, reportedly from the Tudor period as well as two old sweet chestnut trees surviving in gardens on the Estate (and giving a lot of work to their owners!) that could well date back to the end of this period. There is little else that has come to light to date.

Now we move to a time when Blendon features prominently in the nation's financial and religious affairs.

Fig 13. Mulberry Tree at 17 The Sanctuary. A small pond can be seen on the left – the last remnants of the top lake

Fig 14. Sweet Chestnut Tree in Beechway

Chapter Three

Heroes and Villains – the early eighteenth century

In 1732 John Brett Fisher died. He bequeathed Blendon Estate to his son-in-law, Jacob Sawbridge.

On to the Blendon stage comes one of the most interesting characters in eighteenth century England. Jacob Sawbridge, a Director of the South Sea Company, was, for a while, also one of the most reviled. He was placed in custody by the Houses of Parliament and must have seriously feared for his life during the dark days of 1720 and 1721.

Lord Molesworth, who had suffered as a result of the actions of Sawbridge and others said:

> "They ought, on this occasion, follow the example of the ancient Romans, who, having no law against parricide, because their legislators supposed no son could be so unnaturally wicked as to imbue his hands in his father's blood, made a law to punish this heinous crime as soon as it was committed. They adjudged the guilty wretch to be sewn into a sack and thrown alive into the Tiber … and he [Molesworth] should be satisfied to see [the South-Sea Company Directors] tied in a sack and thrown in the Thames."

So who was Sawbridge – and how did he become so notorious?

Jacob Sawbridge (c 1665-1748) of Olantigh, Kent and Hackney, Middlesex came from a Warwickshire family but was actually born in Canterbury. His father had been in business in London and a relative was a bookseller whose premises Jonathan Swift frequented. Sawbridge married Elizabeth Fisher in 1698 and he would have been a frequent visitor to the Blendon Estate before and after that date. In 1715 he became an MP for Cricklade but in 1721 he was expelled from Parliament and heavily fined for his business dealings.[49] By the time he inherited the Estate, in 1731, he had passed from the national stage into relative obscurity. The Sawbridge family connection with Blendon lasted into the latter part of the eighteenth century. It is Sawbridge's business dealings that bring him to prominence – or notoriety – and which we need to examine.

In Burke's 'Landed Gentry' Sawbridge's character is described as 'not a strong one … but what he lacked in will-power he made up in intelligence and activity.'[50] Defoe referred to him, along with Elias Turner and George Caswall, (the two other leaders of the Sword Blade Company [*see over*]), as 'the three

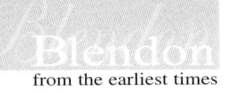

Heroes and Villains – the early eighteenth century

The Brett/Sawbridge connection

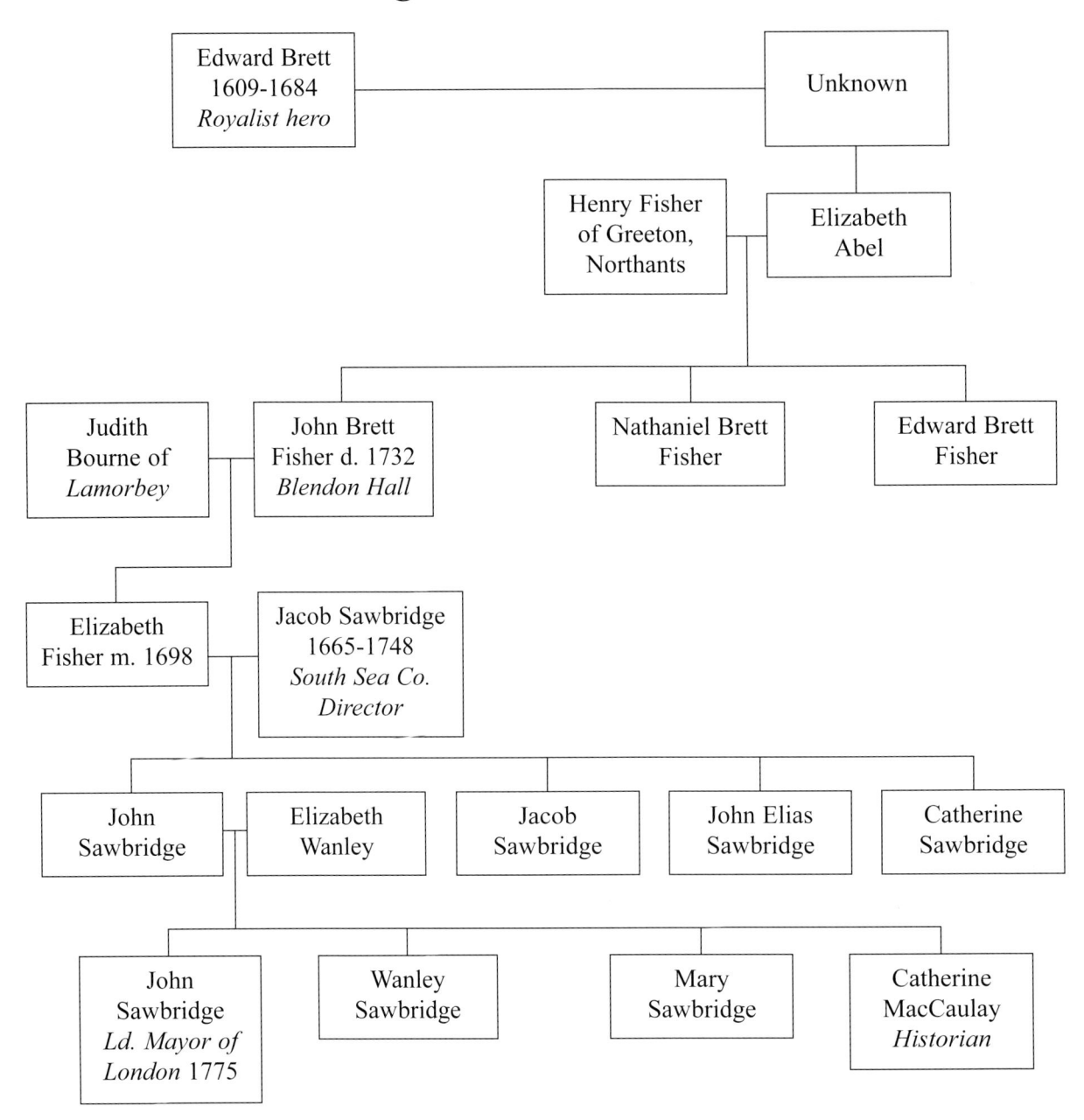

```
Edward Brett 1609-1684 Royalist hero ── Unknown
                                            │
              Henry Fisher of Greeton, Northants ── Elizabeth Abel
                                            │
    ┌────────────────┬──────────────────┬──────────────┐
Judith Bourne   John Brett Fisher   Nathaniel Brett   Edward Brett
of Lamorbey ── d. 1732 Blendon Hall    Fisher           Fisher
        │
Elizabeth Fisher m. 1698 ── Jacob Sawbridge 1665-1748 South Sea Co. Director
        │
    ┌──────────┬────────────┬──────────┬──────────────┬──────────────┐
John       Elizabeth     Jacob       John Elias    Catherine
Sawbridge ── Wanley     Sawbridge    Sawbridge     Sawbridge
        │
    ┌──────────┬────────────┬──────────────┬──────────────┐
John Sawbridge    Wanley       Mary          Catherine
Ld. Mayor of     Sawbridge    Sawbridge     MacCaulay
London 1775                                  Historian
```

Fig 15. The Brett/Sawbridge Connection.

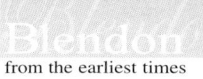

Heroes and Villains – the early eighteenth century

capital sharpers of Britain'. Defoe continued: 'Sawbridge is as cunning as Caswall is bold, and the reserve of one with the openness of the other makes a complete Exchange Alley man…Turner acts in concert. …and makes a complete triumvirate of thieving.' And in many ways Sawbridge's described disposition fits nicely with the way business and commerce was changing at the time. A group of businesses were building up in the area in and around Exchange Alley, in the City of London, which epitomised the growth of a new financial class. With them, or as a prompt to their development, came the business patents and joint stock companies. Joint stock companies exploited the ideas and opportunities presented by patents. With them came stockjobbers. A stockjobber was seen as the person who would most likely fleece the innocent of his money with his patter and promotions.[51]

Fig 16. Exchange Alley at the time of the South Sea Bubble

The Sword Blade

It was into this burgeoning and uncertain world of commercial growth and exploitation that Sawbridge enters in the 1690s. We see him first as one of a syndicate of four who ran a company called the 'Sword Blade Company'. Originally this was a company set up to manufacture European 'hollow blades' – an alternative and preferred weapon to the heavier English sword. The Company was to make its money by importing French Huguenot technicians into the north of England and setting up their production foundry there.

However, by the turn of the century, the Sword Blade Company was trading in a very different sphere of business – very much in the tradition of 'Exchange Alley'

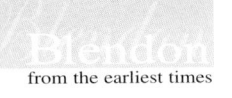

Heroes and Villains – the early eighteenth century

(Interestingly it still produced swords until 1713). In its new guise, the Sword Blade Company became very active in the purchase of properties confiscated from the defeated Jacobite rebels in Ireland and by 1702, it had acquired estates worth a rent-roll of £20,000 a year. Because of its original charter, as a joint-stock company, it had the right to issue stock in exchange for Army Debentures – the paper issued by the Paymaster of the Forces in payment for supplies.

It is almost certain that the syndicate members, Jacob Sawbridge among them, bought Army Debentures as private individuals before the offer was made public and were able to sell this stock to the market as the price rose. It is alleged that this 'insider dealing' meant that individual syndicate members, including Sawbridge, would have made many thousands of pounds as a result of this by the summer of 1703.[52]

However, the financial world is never static and the Sword Blade's fortunes began to turn. The newly established Bank of England had observed the emergence of the Sword Blade Company, with its charter privileges of holding land and issuing stock, with growing anxiety and as a land corporation, and also as a land bank it threatened the position of the Bank. For the next three years Bank and Sword Blade vied for dominance. It culminated in the Bank's victory in which its charter confirmed the Bank's privileges and prohibited any other group from issuing bank notes. The Sword Blade had been stopped and its Irish venture was now not going well as a result of disputes over title of confiscated land and costly lawsuits. By 1708 Sword Blade stock had dropped to fifty-one points and as a result, once wealthy Sword Blade partners almost went bankrupt. Angry and disillusioned, Sword Blade partners blamed the Bank.[53] The scene was now set for the South Sea venture, for which the Sword Blade could be seen as a "practice run" in the uncertain world of City commerce.

We can imagine Sawbridge during the ups and downs of the Sword Blade venture visiting his new in-laws at Blendon. We can perhaps picture him standing pensively in the rooms or walking the corridors of the old Hall or perhaps strolling thoughtfully through the grounds; turning over in his mind the latest machinations of the Sword Blade and its rivals. How much of this he shared with wife or in-laws we can only guess. We can only surmise as to whether he shielded them from the whole business world or gave some 'tips' to John Brett Fisher. Brett Fisher was certainly a wealthy man – how much of this was 'old' money and how much was 'new' is an intriguing question.

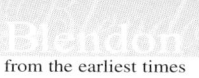

Heroes and Villains – the early eighteenth century

The South Sea Bubble

So what was the South Sea Company and the 'bubble' that eventually burst, creating so much anger and grief? And where did the Sword Blade Company fit into this story – and what was Sawbridge's role in all this? We need to understand what was happening at the very top of English politics in England in 1710 to understand all this.

In 1710 Robert Harley took over as Chancellor of the Exchequer and by May 1711 had become Lord High Treasurer. His accession signalled the end of the Spanish War of Succession or 'Marlborough's War' as it has been called which had been caused by disagreement over the possible extension of French power into Spain. Harley, being a 'new broom', was keen to deliver a peace dividend to reinforce his position. He received numerous approaches and amongst them was the South Sea scheme. It was presented to him by John Blunt, secretary of the Sword Blade Company and enthusiastically encouraged by George Caswall – another Sword Blade member – and a political ally of Harley's from Leominster. Sawbridge would have been busy in his active support.

Fig 17. South Sea House, London

In one brilliant stroke the scheme brought together Harley's passion for a peace dividend, expansion of successful overseas trade and removal of fears about the National Debt – a new phenomenon created to finance the Nine Years War. It also brought together the ways of Exchange Alley and the highest levels of politics and society.

Robert Harley therefore presented this scheme to Parliament in May 1711 and successfully carried it through to establishing the South Sea Company. [54]

So what exactly was the South Sea scheme? The South Sea Trading Company was set up as a joint stock company. As a result, it provided a useful 'repository' for the National Debt, which stood at £9 million in 1711. The scheme meant that unfunded government securities would be compulsorily exchanged for shares in the new company. At a stroke, the National Debt was

Heroes and Villains – the early eighteenth century

removed – and the company was guaranteed an annual income of £568,279.10 by statute (six per cent interest on the debt).

Secondly, the company was also given a monopoly of trade into South America – which as a result of the ending of hostilities with Spain, promised, it was believed, huge benefits. The Treaty of Utrecht in 1713, which had brought the war formally to an end, gave Britain the right to export goods (i.e. slaves) to the Spanish Colonies in South America. The Government vested this right in the South Sea Company and issued shares to its own bondholders in lieu of their investment.

Thirdly, the scheme needed backing – high-level support. The Sword Blade bank handled the bulk of the business. Government departments put forward a substantial sum and about 200 'names' also contributed. Harley himself converted £8,000 worth of securities – probably to ensure that he became Governor of the Company. Blunt, Caswall and Sawbridge and others converted over £65,000. We can guess that even if part of these holdings of Debt had been recently acquired, the personal profits would have been huge. Sawbridge, as one of the Sword Blade group, also gained a directorship of the new company. However, in common with all the other 30 or so directors of the Company, Sawbridge had absolutely no experience of South American trade.[55]

Not that it mattered. As Blunt and his colleagues knew, the South Sea Company's privileges would be used as a front to manipulate financial operations at the highest levels. Just like the Sword Blade, whose charter had been used to run a bank, the company would do something different to what it appeared to be.

The Sword Blade was now flourishing – its old rival the Bank was in the doldrums and by 1712 it had taken advantage of a legal loophole to issue bank notes and even buy shares in the Bank – with the associated voting rights. Sawbridge was in the forefront of its activities.

In 1715 the new King George I and the Prince of Wales quickly acquired holdings themselves in the South Sea Company and the latter was appointed Governor. Blunt and Sawbridge must have been delighted. It was royal patronage at the highest level.[56] At the same time Sawbridge had also moved his career forward in a different direction. He was elected as a Whig MP for Cricklade and partnered Sir George Caswall, his colleague in the Sword Blade.[57]

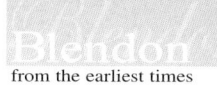

Heroes and Villains – the early eighteenth century

Within two years of his accession, George I had fallen out with his son, the Prince of Wales. As a result in early 1718 the King was elected Governor of the South Sea Company in place of the Prince. This royal tiff did not affect the real controllers of the Company – the Sword Blade syndicate. Caswall, like Sawbridge, had become an MP – and a knight.

Then at the end of 1718 war broke out again between Great Britain and Spain and as a result the South Sea Company's possessions in South America, valued at £300,000, were seized. Unable to trade, the Company was seen to be what it really was – a finance corporation.[58]

We now need to turn our attention briefly to the financial scene in France. The situation there was to have a dramatic impact on the evolution of the South Sea scheme in London.

John Law, a rich successful Scottish financier, had settled in France and had established the Mississippi Company. Like the Sword Blade and South Sea Companies, this was a front for financial manipulation. Law had successfully persuaded the French Government to agree to the conversion of the country's National Debt into shares in the company. Law was feted and money flooded in from France and abroad for shares in the company and the price of the shares shot up phenomenally.

The impact on London was huge and Law's success was seen as a direct threat to England's prosperity. The Government feared that Law could turn his attention to England with a similar, unstoppable scheme and effectively hijack England's National Debt. Law's success meant that money was flowing out of England at an alarming rate.[59] Something had to be done about England's National Debt – which at 1719 stood at £31 million.

The circumstances were right for an approach by Blunt to the Government about settling the Debt 'once and for all'. Negotiations coincided with the new Parliament in the autumn of 1719.

1720

The South Sea scheme – as hammered out between the Government and company including Sawbridge – was an arrangement between them as follows:

Broadly for every pound of annual expenditure on the Debt of which the Government was relieved, the Company was to receive a pound from the Government. If the operation were a complete success after seven years, the service of the National Debt would be reduced to a level 4 per cent. This would

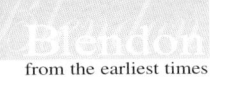

Heroes and Villains – the early eighteenth century

also mean that the Debt would be liquidated in about 25 years. The Company also offered, when the conversion year was over, to make a gift of £3 million to the Exchequer. (The fact that the South Sea had not anywhere near £3 million pounds at its disposal was irrelevant – this was 'futures'.) The arrangement between the Company and the public was more vague – and intentionally so. An equal amount of South Sea stock to the National Debt was to be created in the space of the conversion year and released as fast as the holders of one issue responded. It was not specified how much stock was to be given for a specific amount of Debt – this was left open.[60] The implication of this arrangement was that an inflationary £5 million pounds would be injected into the economy in a very short period of time.

In the winter of 1720, the Bill to facilitate the Scheme, was passing through Parliament. Its passage was being eased by the purchase of 'friendships'. At the same time, anticipation of a scheme that could get you rich quick was stoking up the temperature. It was at this time that Stanhope, Secretary of the Treasury, accepted a promise of £50,000 worth of South Sea stock from Sawbridge. Sawbridge did not actually possess this stock at the time. Sawbridge was also making his personal acquisitions. It is in this year that he purchases Queen Anne, an estate from the Thornhill family at Olantigh near Canterbury.[61]

South Sea stock then began its inevitable climb. In March 1720 it rose from just over 200 points to 320 points. Meanwhile inflation had set in France and Law's scheme was in disarray. But this warning sign was ignored. There were those who warned about the fragility of the scheme – a few even identified that it would go much as it did with 'Devil take the hindmost'. But the speculators held sway and caution and restraint were not the order of the day. The mood was compared to champagne being shaken in a bottle – and the toastmaster was John Blunt.

On 7th April the South Sea Bill gained royal assent and the stock stood at 335 points. John Blunt then came into his own. By a masterful mix of loans and subscriptions, he was able to wind the price of South Sea stock up to 490 points by May. There were some signs of inflation in the economy – land prices had rocketed, as had the price of luxury goods. People had to look to France for a warning of what the future held. Law's scheme was drowning under a tidal wave of inflation. In England meanwhile South Sea trading had become a national contagion. Every one who could wished to be in on it – no one wanted to be left behind. Only the poorest were left out.[62]

Blendon from the earliest times

Heroes and Villains – the early eighteenth century

Fig 18. *The South Sea Scheme* by William Hogarth
(Reproduced by kind permission of the Mary Evans Picture Library)

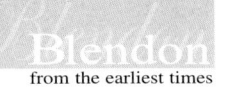

Heroes and Villains – the early eighteenth century

Parallels with Britain's property boom of the late 1980s come to mind. Everyone was urged to buy property for fear of missing out – and property values can only go up – can't they? As a result of this twentieth century collective madness and the resultant bubble the first half of the 1990's was marred and marked by the term 'negative equity' which denoted how your property had reduced in value in relation to your loan. We can perhaps change the metaphor to the children of Hamelin following Blunt – the Pied Piper playing his financial flute with consummate ease. Only the crippled child (the underclass) was left behind.

The first, cleverly managed offer of South Sea stock was made to annuitants (debt holders) in May. The stock value rose at the same time to nearly 500 points. A second loan in June saw the stock jump to 870 points and by July, in the midsummer madness – prices had rocketed to nudging 1000 points. And yet simultaneously in France, paper money was being burnt on bonfires to demonstrate the Government's determination to halt inflation.[63]

People went away for the summer full of optimism. But many thought it could not last, including Chancellor Aislabie, who warned the King not to invest further in the stock. He got a royal reprimand but managed to limit the King's subsequent losses.[64]

The crash came quickly. The immediate cause of the turnabout was a shortage of ready money to pay the annuitants who had converted in May. Blunt, the magical flute player, had lost his touch, and suddenly the happy dance became a danse macabre. In early September, the price of stock slipped dramatically from 870 points to 705 points. By 9th September it was down to 575 points. Blunt's life was under threat and he was subsequently wounded by a disgruntled speculator.

Those people who had been courted widely until very recently were now reviled.

The South Sea Company was provided with a lifeboat … the Bank of England. But there was no room in the lifeboat for the Sword Blade. The Bank was very clear that the Sword Blade could not continue its role if it (the Bank) was to rescue the South Sea Company. So within a week of reopening in September, the Sword Blade shut – promising to pay creditors in due course at 5 per cent interest or in the meantime creditors could have South Sea stock valued at £400 at £100 nominal stock. South Sea stock now stood at 180 points.[65]

But even now things were not as they appeared. The directors of the Sword Blade – Turner, Caswell and Sawbridge had transferred in June 1720 over £1

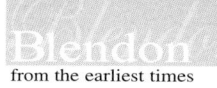

Heroes and Villains – the early eighteenth century

million to a new banking company ostensibly in the names of Knight and Blunt – relatives of the two chief characters of the story. So, even when business appeared to be booming, the syndicate was preparing for rainier days.

The impact of the fall was nationwide. Some bewailed their 'poverty' in comparison to their unrealised 'wealth'. Many others suffered genuine hardship. Sir Isaac Newton, the famous scientist, who had withdrawn from the market in the spring with a profit of £7,000, commenting that he could predict the movement of the stars and planets, but not the madness of people, re-entered the market and lost £20,000 and would never speak of the South Sea Company again. Buildings and ships were left unfinished. Luxury goods were left unpurchased and land deals were left incomplete. By the end of 1720 the word on the streets was that the directors would be hanged and they must at times have feared for their lives. The pressure grew too much for Robert Knight, Cashier of the South Sea Company, who fled to Calais, fearing all would be exposed.

1721 saw retribution. Instead of hanging – a Bill called 'The South Sea Sufferers Bill' was designed to redress the suffering of those who had lost out by penalising South Sea directors. In January 1721 Sawbridge spoke in the Commons, was found guilty of a notorious breach of trust and placed in custody. When Sawbridge was tried for his involvement in the South Sea scheme, he asked the House for leniency on the basis that what he had done 'that may have given offence hath been through ignorance and inadvertency without any private or unlawful views or designs'. He was allowed to keep only £5,000 of a fortune of £77,000, which indicated what the House thought of him.[66] He was also banned from sitting in Parliament or holding public office. The impact of his fall from grace and the loss of such a large amount of money can only be surmised. Clearly he and the Brett Fishers would not have

Fig 19. Sir Isaac Newton - a brilliant scientist but he was tempted to return to the market and fell foul of the South Sea scheme

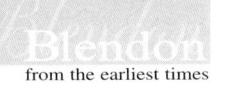

Heroes and Villains – the early eighteenth century

been the people to have at your social function and perhaps he lay low at Canterbury for a while until the heat was off.

Sawbridge died in 1748. He had inherited Blendon in 1732, eleven years after his trial. His descendants included John Sawbridge, a Lord Mayor of London in 1775 (a supporter and successor to John Wilkes the famous libertarian) and the historian Catherine Macaulay (Jacob's granddaughter) who wrote a strong defence of her ancestor.

When we consider the artefacts at Blendon that have come down to us from the first half of the eighteenth century there are three coins from this period that have been found on the Estate in recent years. One is a very well preserved halfpenny found in the grounds of the Bailiff's Cottage (not built at the time) dated 1733. Another coin is a penny found in the Pleasure Grounds (in the area near where the top lake was located) dated 1740 -1745 and the other is a battered coin found in the joists of Jay's cottages dating from the 1730s and apparently placed there to ward off evil spirits.

Historians tell us that these finds from these dates reflect periods of active minting as much as the chance finding of lost coins. However, there is an irony in finding low denomination coinage during the period in which someone, who had been juggling thousands, owned Blendon.

Fig 20. Blendon coins – 18th century

Love's Labours Lost – the 1730s

Brett Fisher died in 1732 and the Hall and Estate passed to Jacob Sawbridge. He was probably in his late sixties by now.

Whilst the 'Bubble' was over a decade before, Sawbridge saw the opportunity to make money from the inheritance. As a result he leased the property out to Thomas Delamotte and his family.

Delamotte was a wealthy London sugar-importer and a Justice of the Peace for Kent. His family, of Huguenot descent, originally came from Tournay in the Low Countries. A sixteenth century ancestor was forced to flee his homeland as a result of persecution by the Spanish under the Duke of Alva. He arrived, penniless, in Southampton in 1586 where he became minister of the French church there.[67]

Thomas Delamotte owned a London home near Fresh Wharf, where his business was located. He and his wife Elizabeth had five children: Charles, William (known as Jacky), Elizabeth (known as Betty), Esther (known as Hetty) and Molly, a much younger daughter.[68]

The Delamottes, and Blendon, were to become intimately involved in early Methodism in England and to become very close to both the Wesleys and George Whitefield.

The first reference to the Delamottes by the Methodists appears in John Wesley's Journal in 1735. He writes:

> "Tuesday, October 14th 1735. Mr Benjamin Ingram of Queens College, Mr Charles Delamotte, son of a merchant in London, my brother Charles and myself took boat for Gravesend in order to embark for Georgia."[69]

Charles and John Wesley are synonymous with the religious revolution in England in the early 18th century. They had founded their 'Holy Club' in Oxford in the 1730s and the term 'Methodist' was originally a sneering criticism of their ordered lives. But Methodism was not destined to be limited to a sleepy university city. Methodism was to be preached (illegally) in the open air and Blendon was to become one of the cradles of Methodism in England and a place in which Charles Wesley, and latterly George Whitefield, would find inspiration and comfort.

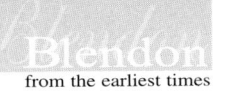

Love's Labours Lost – the 1730s

With the Wesleys came George Whitefield (pronounced 'Whitfield'). Whitefield born in 1714, was an innkeeper's son and slightly younger than the Wesleys. At Oxford, he suffered segregation from the Wesleys because of his class, but by 1733 he was welcomed into the Holy Club.

It was Whitefield who was to prove his power and mastery of preaching – moving vast numbers to tears by his exhortations. The satirists called him 'Mr Squintum' because of his appearance caused by measles as a child. David Garrick, the actor, however said he would give 100 guineas to be able to say 'oh' with such pathos as Whitefield could create. A brilliant satirical cartoon entitled "Credulity, Superstition and Fanaticism" depicting Whitefield's preaching was drawn by William Hogarth, who along with Samuel Johnson, Sir Joshua Reynolds and Oliver Goldsmith and others sneered at Whitefield. Whitefield was once described as: having 'a great voice, a simplicity of manner, dramatic effect, vanity and making constant appeals for money'

Apart from his eloquence, Whitefield promised both heaven and hell to those that listened to him. His was not a cosy religion – he would exhort and rail – and his listeners would weep tears of exultation. Weeping was the trademark of Whitefield's effect on people through his preaching.

Fig 21. John Wesley travelled to Georgia in 1735 and en route met some Moravians who impressed him deeply by their firm belief. Personally the mission to Georgia was not a success, Wesley being sued for £1,000 for defamation of character. He arrived back in England in early 1738 and visited Blendon on his way back from Deal to give the Delamottes news of their son Charles.

Love's Labours Lost – the 1730s

Fig. 22. "Enthusiasm Delineated" or "Credulity, Superstition and Fanaticism" depicting Whitefield's preaching by William Hogarth (Reproduced by kind permission of the Mary Evans Picture Library)

Love's Labours Lost – the 1730s

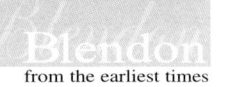

By 1737, Charles Wesley, John's brother, was also already well acquainted with the Delamottes. He visited them for the first time at Blendon in July 1736 and also from time to time at Fresh Wharf in London. Charles Wesley seems to have spent most time with Esther Delamotte (the middle sister who he calls "Hetty" and "simple Hetty" in his journals). In October he records a ride with William ("Jacky") Delamotte and the fact that both of them suffer mishaps – Jacky being 'flung over his horse's head'[70] It was on October 30th 1737 that Elizabeth Delamotte, in the company of her brother, William, and Charles Wesley first heard Whitefield preach. By this time Whitefield was fast approaching 'celebrity status' in London and was unable to travel by foot because of fear of being mobbed by crowds.[71]

You sense that Mr and Mrs Delamotte must have had reservations about the Wesleys, and later Whitefield, and their contact with their family. It was bad enough that one of their sons had been lured away to America for years. Now came the possibility of losing another son in an accident and daughters' heads being turned by Wesley's eloquence. This must have made Mr and Mrs Delamotte quite desperate. In November, there was, what one suspects, one of a number of 'run ins' between the Wesleys and the Delamottes. It occurred when Elizabeth informed Wesley that her mother thought he would 'make Hetty run mad'[72] and therefore the Delamottes sent her away to London from Blendon ahead of Wesley's visit. It was a ploy that did not work as Wesley met her in London instead. He records later in November that Mrs Delamotte was "cold, averse and prejudiced against the truth".[73] But within a week of this, following his preaching at Bexley (12 November 1737) he states 'Mrs Delamotte thanked me for my sermon with tears, owned she had loved Charles too well and was quite altered in her behaviour towards me."[74] Two days later he records: 'Little Molly burst into tears upon my telling her God loved her. The whole family now appear not far from the Kingdom of God.'[75]

Whitefield spent most of 1738 in America. (He would cross the Atlantic thirteen times during his life). In February 1738, John Wesley, having landed at Deal, travelled to Blendon to tell the Delamottes about Charles Delamotte's activities in America. Charles returned to Blendon the following year.

By June 1738 Wesley's powerful influence over the Delamottes resulted in Mrs Delamotte, three of the five children, their minister (the Reverend Henry Piers, Vicar of Bexley), two maidservants and the Blendon gardener being 'converted to Christ'.

We are told that Blendon Hall resounded to vigorous prayer and praise of God.

Love's Labours Lost – the 1730s

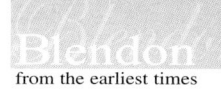

By December 1738 Whitefield had returned to England.[76] He states on his first evening at Blendon:

> 'A happier household have I seldom found. …Rose about five, spent above an hour most agreeably in prayer, singing and reading the Scriptures with the church in Mr Delamotte's house…'[77]

This Blendon Hall building had its own chapel.[78] But Whitefield was attracted to Blendon for other reasons. He had grown fond of Elizabeth Delamotte (the eldest daughter) and she in turn seems to have reciprocated his affection. Whitefield, writing in his journals, never says this in so many words but his description of his time at Blendon reveals that other feelings apart from religious ones were coming in to play.[79] He speaks of Blendon Hall as a 'sweet retreat' and of 'finding heaven on earth'[80] there. His journals have a number of other entries in the late spring and summer of that year that indicate the pull that Blendon had on him. They include:

> **Tuesday June 5th:** I returned to Blendon rejoicing and spent the evening most delightfully with many dear Christian friends……….
>
> **Thursday 7th June:** Here some of Mr Delamotte's family gave us the meeting. After sermon I returned to their house at Blendon….
>
> **Friday June 8th:** I returned to my sweet retreat at Blendon. Oh the comforts of being all of one mind in a house! It begins our heaven upon earth. Were I left to my own choice here would be my rest…
>
> **Sunday June 10th:** Hastened back to Blendon…Dined gave thanks and sang hymns at Mr Delamotte's
>
> **Thursday June 14th:** Spent the whole day in my pleasant and profitable retreat at Blendon
>
> **Sunday August 5th:** Expounded, prayed and sang psalms at Mr Delamotte's door. Preached in the afternoon to about fifteen hundred in Justice Delamotte's yard…
>
> **Tuesday August 7th:** …dined at Blendon
>
> **Sunday August 12th:** Preached early in the morning to some hundreds in Justice Delamotte's yard…Preached at 3 in the afternoon to nearly three thousand in Mr Delamotte's yard…
>
> **Monday August 13th:** Rose early and hastened to Blendon…. Dined and took leave of my dear weeping friends. Rode with many of them to Erith, took my final and sorrowful farewell.[81]

There are also many references to Whitefield preaching at Bexley Church during this time. However, Blendon had also had a practical pull on Whitefield – he needed to be close to the down-river ports as he was anticipating a return to America.

Whitefield's celebrity status had also grown. In June 1739 he spoke to over

Love's Labours Lost – the 1730s

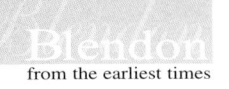

3,000 people who had gathered in the gardens of Blendon Hall and he then went with them to Blackheath, where their numbers swelled to 30,000! Later in the year Benjamin Franklin was to testify scientifically that Whitefield's voice could carry audibly to over 30,000 in the town of Philadelphia.[82]

What we need to consider is the impact his feelings for Elizabeth were having on him. He had not allowed himself (or not found the right person) to experience such desires and had remained 'wedded to Christ' and this was an integral part of his ministry. He had, in the past, exhorted others to be devoted alone to the Lord and expressed views that suggest that a preacher could not share his feelings by having a relationship of such intensity with another person here on earth. There is however, during this period, some evidence from his letters that his view was softening on this issue.

Fig 23. Benjamin Franklin befriended by Whitefield and who became his principal American publisher. Franklin was deeply impressed by Whitefield's speeches and powers of oratory.

This ambivalence of deeply held views created emotional turmoil for Whitefield and he must have given Elizabeth very mixed signals as he wrestled with his spiritual conscience.

Whitefield spent 1740 in America. On his way across the Atlantic he wrote a letter to William Delamotte, Elizabeth's brother, that gives us an insight into his inner conflict:

> "I trust God has enabled you to take the advice that you gave me, and that you have been kept from idolatry. Oh my dear brother let us watch and pray, that we may not be led into temptation. The spirit is willing in both; but the flesh, mine in particular, is exceeding weak…at present my heart is quite free…I endeavour to resign myself wholly to God. I desire His will may be done in me, by me and upon me."[83]

He devoted his time in America to preaching and converting. He followed a

Love's Labours Lost – the 1730s

Fig 24. Whitefield preaching

policy of 'preach and return' and tackled the task with energy and devotion.[84]

Elizabeth sent letters that reached Whitefield in Savannah. Sadly for Whitefield, the torment that he was experiencing is reflected in his letters and his response to Elizabeth mirrors this. He wrote back to her after a few weeks and the relevant elements are set out below:

> "You do well to go about doing good. Your Master did so before you. Dare, dear Miss, to follow his good example . . .
> I beseech you by the mercies of God in Christ Jesus our Saviour, to keep up a close walk and communion with God. Nothing else can preserve you from idols; and you know when once the soul is off its watch, the devil makes sad ravages in it. There is nothing I dread more than having my heart drawn away by earthly objects. - When that time comes, it will be over with me indeed; I must then bid adieu to zeal and fervency of spirit, and in effect bid the Lord Jesus to depart from me. For alas, what room can there be for God, when a rival hath taken possession of the heart?
> Oh my dear Sister, pray that no such evil may befal me. My blood runs cold at the very thought thereof. I cannot, indeed; I cannot away with it.
> In a multiplicity of business, have I wrote you these lines. I thank you for your kind letter, and hope I shall always retain a grateful sense of the many favours I have received from your dear family. My kindest respects attend your sister; I long to

Love's Labours Lost – the 1730s

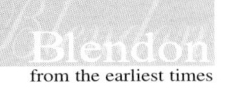

>hear of her being brought into the glorious liberty of the children of God. How does your father?
>Oh that he may have a well-grounded interest in Christ! How does my dear brother Charles - I pray God to fill him with all joy and peace in believing. And how does your little sister? Dearest Redeemer, keep her unspotted from the world!
>My heart is now full. Writing quickens me. I could almost drop a tear, and wish myself, for a moment or two; in England. But hush, nature: God here pours down His blessings on"
>Your sincere friend and servant in Christ,
>G. W[85]

We can only surmise about the confusion that this letter caused Elizabeth. On the one hand is he not saying that she is the earthly object that could distract him from the Lord and yet he also wishes that he were with her in England and the reference to a tear is steeped in symbolism? Did not Whitefield measure his impact on others by moving them to tears in the name of Christ? The ambivalence of his letter must have totally confused Elizabeth.

Whitefield suffered torments as a result of this dichotomy in the following weeks and these are recorded in his Journals where he refers to 'inward trials'. As a result it was there, in America on his way to Philadelphia, that he decided to propose marriage to her.

However, his marriage proposal came in the form of an offer to Elizabeth to manage the affairs of the orphan house in Bethesda and marriage was a secondary element in the proposition.

He wrote two letters. One addressed to Mr and Mrs Delamotte and with it he enclosed the other to be passed to Elizabeth, if they agreed.

They are as follows:

>April 4, 1740
>My DEAR FRIENDS,
>Since I wrote last, we have buried our Sister L-. Rachel I left at Philadelphia, and sister T- seems to be in a declining state; so that sister A- alone is like to be left of all the women which came over with me from England. I find by experience, that a mistress is absolutely necessary for the due management of my increasing family, and to take off some of that care, which at present lies upon me. Besides, I shall in all probability, at my next return from England, bring more women with me: and I find, unless they are all truly gracious (or indeed if they are) without a superior, matters cannot be carried on as becometh the Gospel of Jesus Christ.
> It hath been therefore much impressed upon my heart that I should marry; in order to have a help meet for me in the work whereunto our dear Lord Jesus hath called me. This comes (like Abraham's servant to Rebekah's relations) to know whether you think your daughter, Miss E-, is a proper person to engage in such an

Love's Labours Lost – the 1730s

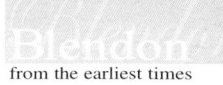

undertaking? If so, whether you will be pleased to give me leave to propose marriage unto her? You need not be afraid of sending me a refusal. For, I bless God, if I know anything of my own heart, I am free from that foolish passion which the world calls Love. I write only because I believe it is the will of God that I should alter my state; but your denial will fully convince me, that your daughter is not the person appointed by God for me. He knows my heart; I would not marry but for Him, and in Him, for ten thousand worlds. - But I have sometimes thought

Miss E- would be my help-mate; for she has often been impressed upon my heart. I should think myself safer in your family, because so many of you love the Lord Jesus, and consequently would be more watchful over my precious and immortal soul.

After strong cryings and tears at the throne of grace for direction, and after unspeakable troubles with my own heart, I write this. Be pleased to spread the letter before the Lord; and if you think this motion to be of him, be pleased to deliver the inclosed to your daughter

- If not, say nothing, only let me know you disapprove of it, and that shall satisfy, dear Sir and Madam,

your obliged friend and servant in Christ,

G. W[86]

The letter for Elizabeth reads as follows:

April 4, 1740

Be not surprised at the contents of this: - The letter sent to your honoured father and mother will acquaint you with the reasons.

Do you think you could undergo the fatigues, that must necessarily attend being joined to one, who is every day liable to be called out to suffer for the sake of Jesus Christ? Can you bear to leave your father and kindred's house, and to trust on Him, (who feedeth the young ravens that call upon Him) for your own and children's support, supposing it should please Him to bless you with any? Can you undertake to help a husband in the charge of a family, consisting perhaps of a hundred persons? Can you bear the inclemencies of the air both as to cold and heat in a foreign climate? Can you, when you have a husband, be as though you had none, and willingly part with him, even for a long season, when his Lord and Master shall call him forth to preach the Gospel, and command him to leave you behind - If after seeking to God for direction, and searching your heart, you can say 'I can do all those things through Christ strengthening me' what if you and I were joined together in the Lord, and you came with me at my return from England, to help meet for me in the management of the orphan-house? I have a great reason to believe it is the divine will that I should alter my condition, and have often thought that you was the person appointed for me. I shall still wait on God for direction, and heartily entreat Him, that if this motion be not of Him, it may come to nought.

I write thus plainly, because, I trust, I write not from any other principles but the love of God. - I shall make it my business to call on the Lord Jesus, and would advise you to consult both Him and your friends - For in order to attain a blessing; We should call both the Lord Jesus and His disciples to the marriage…………

I make no great profession to you, because I believe you think me sincere. The

Love's Labours Lost – the 1730s

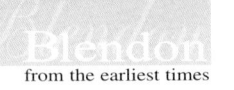

passionate expressions which carnal courtiers use, I think, ought to be avoided by those that would marry in the Lord. I can only promise by the help of God, 'to keep my matrimonial vow, and to do what I can towards helping you forward in the great work of your salvation'. If you think marriage will be in any way prejudicial to your better part, be so kind as to send me a denial. I would not be a snare to you for the world. You need not be afraid of speaking your mind. I trust, I love you only for God, only by His command and for His sake and desire to be joined to you

With fear and much trembling I write, and shall patiently tarry the Lord's leisure, till He is pleased to incline you, dear Miss-, to send an answer to,
Your affectionate brother, friend and servant in Christ,
G. W[87]

When Whitefield reached Philadelphia he sent these letters and waited the four months for a reply for trans-Atlantic correspondence. Whilst clearly sincere, in the art of persuasion he could not have got it more wrong if he had tried. Charles Delamotte, Elizabeth's brother, had already gone off to America and Mr and Mrs Delamotte would have felt that they had lost him in the distant colony for a number of years. His father had tried to buy Charles off from the adventure in 1735 and now five years on, the spectre of losing their daughter to the same place – and possibly for good - must have galvanised them into action. There is an intriguing reference in 1740 referring to Elizabeth being removed from her father's will[88] so we can guess the sort of response Whitefield's letter would have evoked. Here was Whitefield asking for Elizabeth to join him in America to succeed a woman he had brought from England who had already died!

There were also other factors at work. By the time Whitefield's letters arrived, the Delamottes, along with many other members of the Fetter Lane Society, had converted to the Moravians, a rival religious sect. This included Charles who had been with the Wesleys in America. This was ironic for Whitefield who, whilst in America, had done an act of great kindness to the impoverished Moravians living in Philadelphia. There had however been a serious schism with Wesley and his United Societies movement, so much so that when Wesley visited Blendon in June 1740 he wrote:

'I went thence to Blendon: no longer Blendon to me. They could hardly force themselves to be barely civil. I took a hasty leave, and with a heavy heart, weighted down by ingratitude, returned to Bexley.'[89]

Not only this. There was another suitor for Elizabeth. William Holland was a successful tradesman, and also a Moravian. He had been reading from Luther the night John Wesley was converted. Holland proposed to her so that she had a choice between Holland and Whitefield. Whitefield received his reply four months after his original despatch and his reference to the reply in a letter to

Love's Labours Lost – the 1730s

William Seward is as follows:

"I find from Blendon letters that Miss E- D- is in a seeking state only. Surely that will not do. I would have one that is full of faith and the Holy Ghost. Just now I have been weeping and much carried out in prayer before the Lord. My poor family gives me more concern than everything else put together. I want a gracious woman that is dead to everything but Jesus . . . I wait upon the Lord every moment . . . and He assures me He will not permit me to fall by the hands of a woman . . . Looking back upon the workings of my heart in this affair, I am more and more convinced it is of God - and therefore know that He will order things for me as will best promote His own glory. So that my dear Lord's honour does not suffer, I care not what trouble in the flesh I undergo."[90]

However, Captain Gladman reported back the Delamottes' thoughts and caused Whitfield to write on November 25 to Gilbert Tennent:

'Mr and Mrs Delamotte refuse to give their daughter, but yet I believe she may be my wife'[91]

The door was not completely closed on Whitefield but by the time he returned

Fig 25. Charleston where Whitefield faced hostility for, amongst other things, supporting slaves

Love's Labours Lost – the 1730s

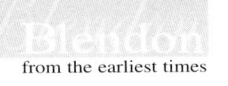

to England (in March 1741), Elizabeth and William Holland were about to be married.

There is only one final reference to the Delamottes in Whitefield's works – over twelve years later and he claims they are still friends. And one other reference, when in writing to a young man who has been refused marriage to the woman he loved, where Whitefield states:

'My affair went as yours but I was called upon to sacrifice my Rachel!'[92]

There is however a happy postscript for Whitefield. In November 1741 he married a Welsh widow, Mrs Elizabeth James and after two years they had a son, John. Whitefield had over twenty-five years with Elizabeth – she died in 1768 and he passed on, to be with Christ, in September 1770.

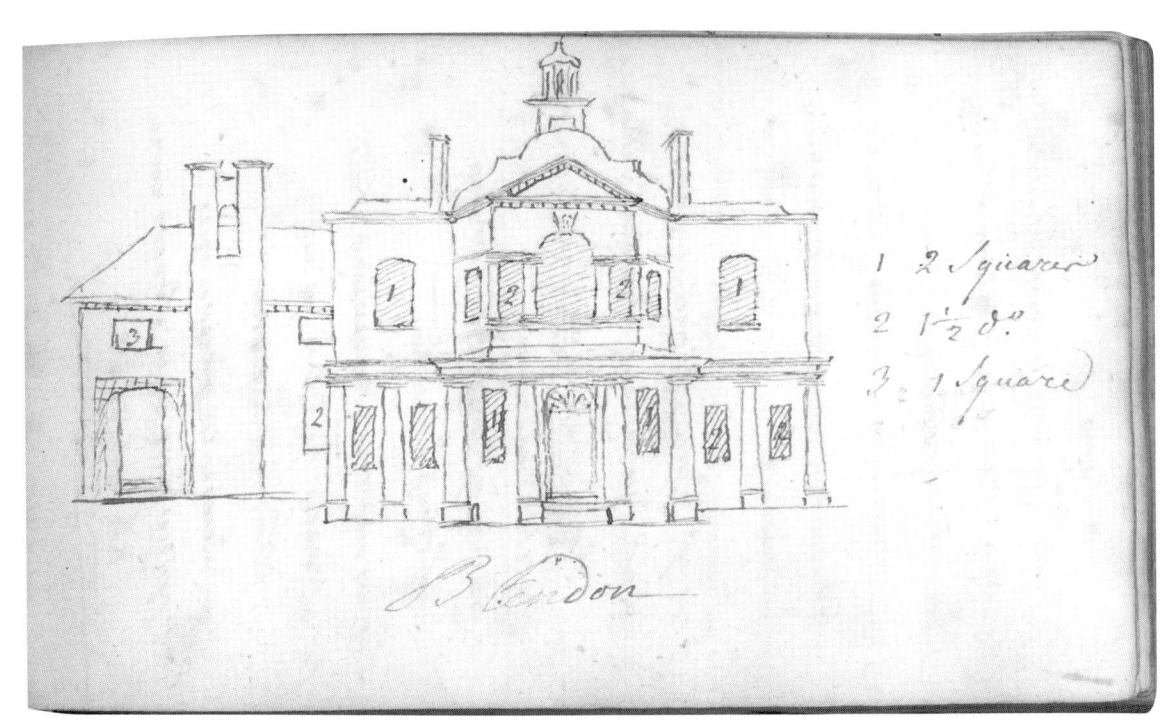

Blendon Hall c1751. This was the building that George Whitefield and the Wesleys knew and was home to the Delamotte family. Reproduced by kind permission of Stoke on Trent Archive Service and Mr Anthony Littleton, the owner of the document.

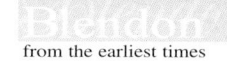

The end of the Sawbridge connection and the building of the new hall – 1763-1807

In the second half of the eighteenth century there is no Sawbridge or Whitefield to write about at Blendon – but there are events to intrigue and interest us and at the end of the century a very interesting occupant.

The major event at Blendon during this period is the building of the new hall – Lady Mary Scott's 'neat mansion' as Hasted describes it in his journal of the late 1770s.[93] For large landowners the eighteenth century was a period of intense building activity. They wanted to augment and improve their estates to pass on to their heirs. On Blendon's northern border, John Boyd was re-building Danson Mansion of Portland stone a quarter of a mile away from the original building. Work commenced in 1763. Boyd employed Robert Taylor, the architect of the Bank of England, to design the new building and also Nathaniel Richmond, a pupil of Lancelot 'Capability' Brown, to landscape the grounds.[94]

This period also gives us the first detailed maps of Blendon. There is the 1766 map which shows both Lady Mary Scott's and William Scott's lands 'purchased of Jacob Sawbridge Esq.' William was Mary's brother in law – her dead husband's brother. We also have the 1783 map that shows the proposed new footpath across the west and south of the estate.

In the early 1760's Jacob Sawbridge (second son of the 'South Sea' Jacob Sawbridge, who had died in 1748) had been leasing out the estate to the Hon. Colonel Desaguliers. Thomas Desaguliers had been the Chief Firemaster in the Royal Artillery since 1748 (succeeding James Pattison – see below). Desaguliers had joined the Royal Artillery in 1740 as a cadet gunner and by 1757 he was made Lieutenant Colonel and in 1761 he became a Colonel. In the same year he commanded the Royal Artillery at the reduction of Belleisle on the west coast of France during the Seven Years War against the French. A manuscript journal of that siege, which is attributed to him, is in the Royal Artillery Library at Woolwich.

Colonel Desaguliers invented a method of projecting between 400 and 600 small shot from mortars. He also undertook many experiments for the construction of rockets.

He was the first artilleryman to be made a Fellow of the Royal Society and his

The end of the Sawbridge connection

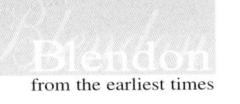

name is still remembered in Royal Gun Factories today – 'Desaguliers' Instrument' being used for examining and verifying the bores of cannon. This instrument only became obsolete with the disappearance of small-bore ordnance.[95]

In February 1765 Sawbridge leased the estate to 'Lady Mary Scott of Sedcop, in the parish of Foots Cray' and then sold it to her the following day for £3,200 (this was the lease and release device for selling property at the time).[96] Lady Mary Scott then took out a loan from Sir William Dolben of Thingdon in Northamptonshire for £1,678 7s.[97]

Lady Mary Scott had not had an easy life. By the time she bought Blendon she had buried two husbands and was bringing up her only daughter from the first marriage. Mary Scott was one of Charles Crompton's four daughters who in turn was the fourth son of George, the fourth Earl of Northampton. She first married Richard Haddock, son of Admiral Haddock, by whom she conceived Mary. Then in 1751 she married Arthur Scott, of North Upton, Commissioner of Chatham Yard and a younger son of the Scotts of Scott's – Hall. He died in 1756. She had however received, by special favour, the rank and precedence of an earl's daughter, which gave her the title of 'Lady'.[98]

Hasted states that Mary Scott "erected on the 'feite' (site) a neat mansion and much improved the park and grounds about it."[99] Whether Hasted means that she erected the new building on the site of the old hall or on the site of the estate – we do not know. When exactly she did this during her residence is difficult to say – but there are some clues.

In 1762 and 1764 the rental value on Blendon, on which Land Tax was based, was constant at £30 per annum. (Land Tax was levied at 4 shillings in the pound and helped pay for the French wars.) When Lady Mary Scott took over the Hall and estate, the rental value had risen to £36 per annum in 1767 and was the same in 1771. It is possible that acquisition of further land, or the split of the land between William and Mary when purchased from Sawbridge, could have prompted this increase or it may be an indicator of the value of the new Hall.[100] We also have records of Window Tax for the years 1766, 1767 and 1771, in which the number of windows for Blendon Hall (this would include outbuildings) was constant at 58.[101] Clearly, rebuilding the Hall would have taken some time to complete. Boyd's mansion at Danson took five years to complete – but he was starting from scratch on a new site and during the period his first wife died and he remarried.[102] Blendon was possibly slightly larger than Danson but not built to the same grand design. Whilst Danson was built of Portland stone, Blendon was made of brick and stucco. We also do not know

The end of the Sawbridge connection

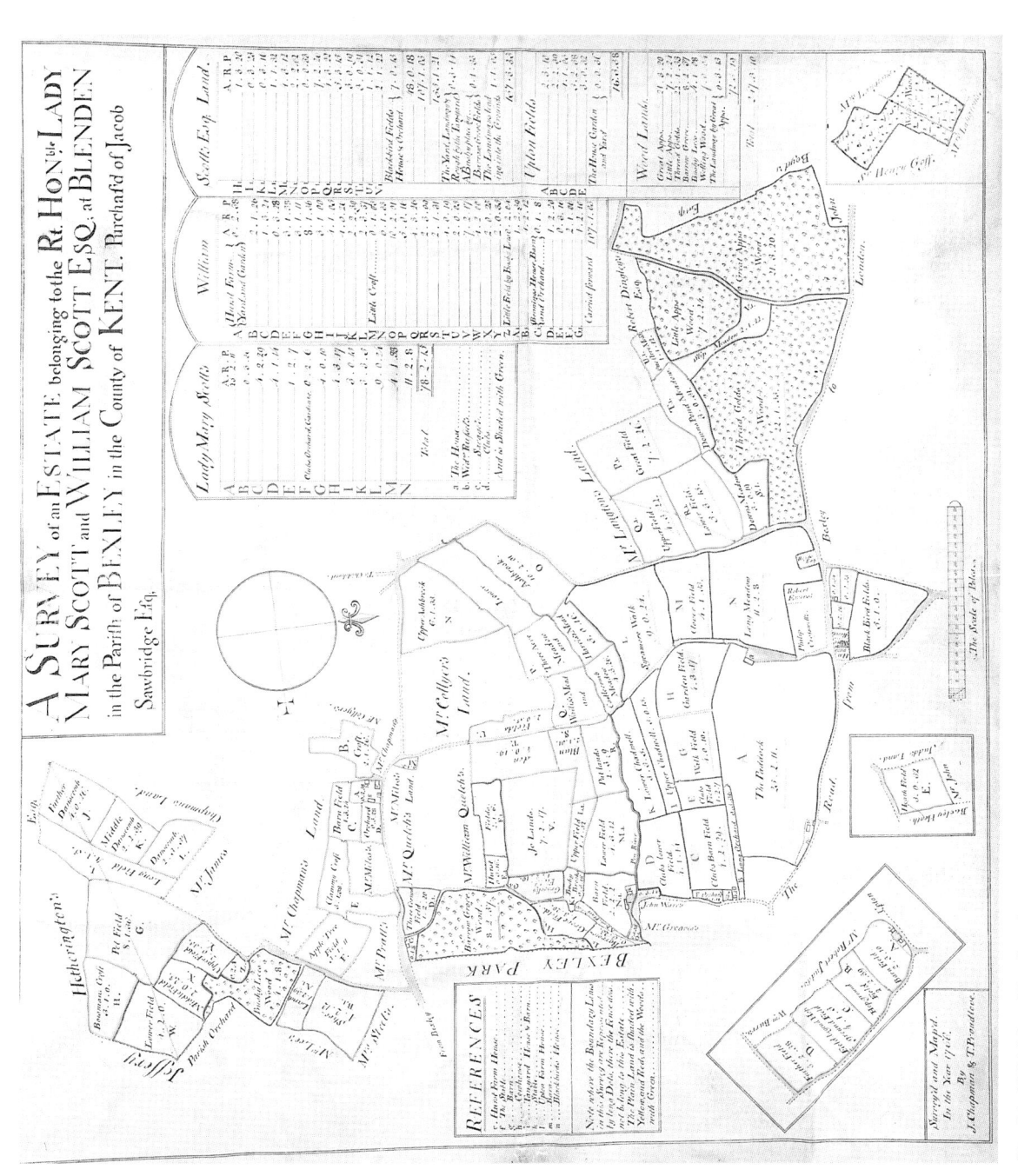

Fig 26. 1766 Map. The first known extant map showing detail of Blendon.
(Reproduced by the kind permission of The Centre for Kentish Studies in Maidstone, Kent)

The end of the Sawbridge connection

who the architect was at Blendon – he was probably a journeyman designer whose name is lost to us. The indicators therefore point to 1765 -1766 as the likely period in which the Hall was built. This brings us to our first extant map of the Estate. This map was originally in the possession of Beverley Nunn, the Sidcup historian who deposited it at the Centre for Kentish Studies in Maidstone and this was brought to our attention by Malcolm Barr-Hamilton, formerly archivist at the Local Studies and Archive Centre at Hall Place, Bexley.[103]

The map dates from 1766 and shows both William and Mary's estate. The estate is viewed from the north/north-east, with 'Black Bird Fields' and the road from Bexley at the bottom and Hurst Farm and adjoining lands at the top. In total, Lady Mary's lands were over 78 acres, but William's are much larger, totalling almost 250 acres – including land at Upton.

The map raises a number of issues. The first one, from the aspect of our story, is whether we are looking at a map incorporating the old or the new Hall. Also we can see that the approach to the Hall is from the north – approximately where Beechway is today. Secondly, there are no lakes shown – although the River Shuttle appears as Pen River. We can also see some dwellings at Bridgen and also in Tanyard Lane (now Elmwood Drive). Family names that appear in the map include Savage, Russell and Club, Crosweller and Ewers; Harman, Reeves and Ware.

Also in 1766 we have a document that records the approval by the Archbishop of Canterbury for the appropriation of pews in the north aisle at St Mary's Church to Lady Mary Scott, her family and servants.[104]

Lady Mary Scott died on 8th May 1782, aged only 53 and was buried at Bexley. She left the estate to her brother-in-law William and was survived by her daughter, Mary Haddock, who had not married. In November of that year, the estate and Hall was leased and released by Mary Haddock of Welbeck Street to General James Pattison of the Royal Artillery, who remained in residence until the early nineteenth century.[105]

Pattison had a long and distinguished career in the Royal Artillery. He was born at Burrage House, Plumstead and joined the Royal Artillery as a cadet in 1739[106] and by 1761 had risen to Lieutenant Colonel. He commanded the companies of the Royal Artillery in Portugal in 1762 towards the end of the Seven Years War.[107] In 1769 he was sent to Venice to superintend the organisation of the Venetian artillery. He commanded the Royal Artillery during the latter part of the American War of Independence and was Commandant of New York. (See Appendix I for a description of his time there) He was twice Commandant of

The end of the Sawbridge connection

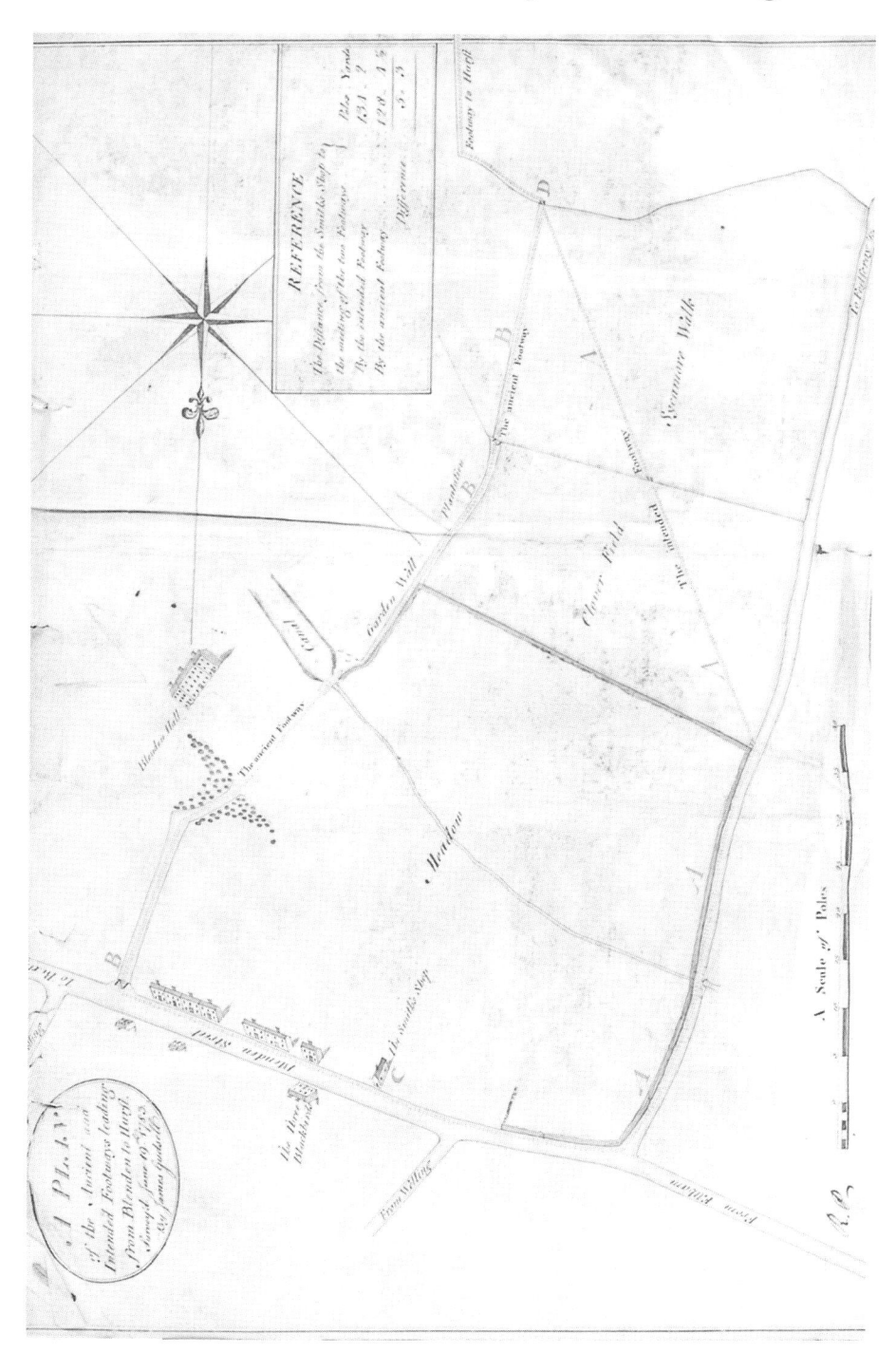

Fig 27. James Gudsell Map of 1783. This includes Lady Mary Scott's 'neat mansion'. Note the original pitched roof *(Bexley Local Studies)*

The end of the Sawbridge connection

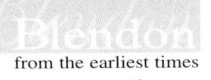

Fig 28. General James Pattison. See Appendix I - Pattison's time in New York as Commandant in the American War of Independence. Pattison was a respected soldier – admired both by his staff and men and by the authorities he had to deal with.
(Courtesy of Greenwich Local Studies, Blackheath)

Woolwich Garrison (1787 and 1788) and was also Governor of the Royal Military Academy, Woolwich.[108] He eventually became a General in 1797 – after fifty-five years of service.[109]

In 1795 Pattison is also listed as a stockholder of the East India Company and entitled to one vote – which meant he would have had a stock of £1,000. In 1806 his sons or heirs are also listed as having two votes between them in the same company. There is an ironic symmetry that for Blendon the beginning of the century should be marked by someone who was associated with financial manipulation and ends with someone associated with a highly respectable and successful trading organisation.

The end of the Sawbridge connection

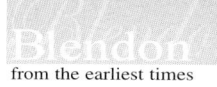

Other events worthy of mention that we know of in this period are:

In 1783 Sir John Boyd at Danson sold a messuage (dwelling), shop and garden to Pattison, which had been formerly occupied by Robert Stephens, wheelwright. Boyd also sold to Pattison a barn, outhouse and yard originally occupied by Thomas Vale and then by his widow. Boyd had recently bought this from Thomas Pearne.[110] However, Sir John Boyd was not the acquisitive man of former years. His fortunes had dipped dramatically and we may interpret this deal as a small contribution to the debts that he was trying to clear at this time.

In 1783 we also see all the title deeds and legal documents relating to Blendon Hall being copied. This may be for the very practical reason that the total estate was being split between William Scott and General Pattison and both parties would require a copy. Finally, there is the 1783 map.[111] This forms part of an order for the stopping of an ancient footway from Blendon to Hurst and giving it another direction. It is dated 30 June 1783 based on a survey by James Gudsell on 19 June and bears an interesting comparison with the 1766 map.

The 1783 map (Fig. 27) shows the relative distances from the Smiths' shop (in Blenden Street) compared to the point at which they would meet on the southern boundary of the estate. The ancient footway goes east along Blenden Street (today's Blendon Road), enters the estate approximately at a point at the northern end of today's Beechway and then proceeds south/south-west towards the Hall and then veers south-west to cross the stream that feeds the canal (the 'top' lake between The Sanctuary and The Drive of later maps) and then continues south-west with the garden wall on its left, separating the plantation on the east and Meadow, Clover Field and Sycamore Walk on the west.

The intended footpath starts by going west along Blenden Street, turns left into what is now Penhill Road and then cuts south-east into the estate at border of the Meadow and Clover Field and goes in a straight line across Sycamore Walk to join the entrance/exit point on the southern boundary of the estate. The intended footway is five poles (a pole is five and a half yards) longer than the ancient one, but its intention is clear – to keep people away from the Hall. Pattison clearly did not want all and sundry standing to gawp at his nice new hall. What else can we see from this map? We have some of the same field names as in the 1766 map – Clover Field and Sycamore Walk, but Long Meadow has become Meadow. There also appears to be a footbridge over the stream that feeds the 'canal' – an early name for the top lake. It is also tempting to suggest that the 'Smiths Shop' is part of the property that Boyd was to sell to Pattison later in the year. We can also see 'The Three Blackbirds' and properties standing where Jay's Cottages are today.

The end of the Sawbridge connection

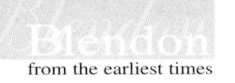

But most intriguing of all is the 'drawing' of Blendon Hall. Here we can see a classic Georgian building showing the characteristic three sections of the Hall and pitched roof that was to disappear thirty-five years later when it was Gothicised. Perhaps this is our one and only glimpse of Lady Mary Scott's 'neat mansion' as it was originally designed.

Fig 29. Bricks from the Hall. These bricks have been found in Beechway and date from the eighteenth century and include coving bricks.

Chapter Six

The Smiths – Part I – Bankers and Builders 'Tenax in Fide' – 1807–1824

In the autumn of 1807, Blendon Hall changed hands again. General James Pattison, who had owned the estate since 1783, had died on 1st March 1805 in London. He is buried in Plumstead churchyard.[112] His heirs retained the property until 1807 and then sold it to the banker, John Smith.[113]

In some ways we know more about Smith and his time at the Hall than any other occupant until the Jays at the end of the century. The reason for this is that John Smith was a serving MP and we have his voting record in the House of Parliament throughout the period. We also have the changes that he instigated whilst living at the Hall and Repton's brief description of the Hall and grounds. Again, however, we know we are missing drawings and maps, extant at the time, which would tell us so much more.

So who was 'plain' John Smith? John Smith was the sixth son of Abel Smith, a Nottingham banker, who had jointly founded the banking firm of Smith, Payne and Smith in 1758. This became the National Provincial Bank in 1924. John's brothers included George, Robert and Samuel, all of whom were to become MPs. Since 1799, John was the joint partner at the London branch of the bank with his elder brother George.[114] John Smith acquired Blendon aged just forty. He was in his second marriage. He had originally married Sarah Boone, daughter of Thomas Boone, Commissioner of Customs, in 1793. Sadly, she died in the following year. In January 1800, Smith married again – this time to Elizabeth Tucker, daughter of Lieutenant Colonel Martin Tucker, by whom he had two sons.[115] These were uncertain times in England, with the news of the developing revolution in France dominating the last decade of the eighteenth century. The rise of Bonaparte with his imperialist aspirations brought the country to war. In 1798, Smith is registered as a Volunteer in the London and Westminster light horse. In 1802, he was returned as MP for Wendover by his eldest brother, Robert, Lord Carrington.[116] The Smiths took the ennobled name of 'Carrington' because of the fictional medieval story of Sir Michael Carrington, who, having committed a misdemeanour, assumed the name of 'Smith' to cover his tracks.

The Smiths – Part I

Smiths the Bankers

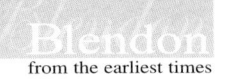

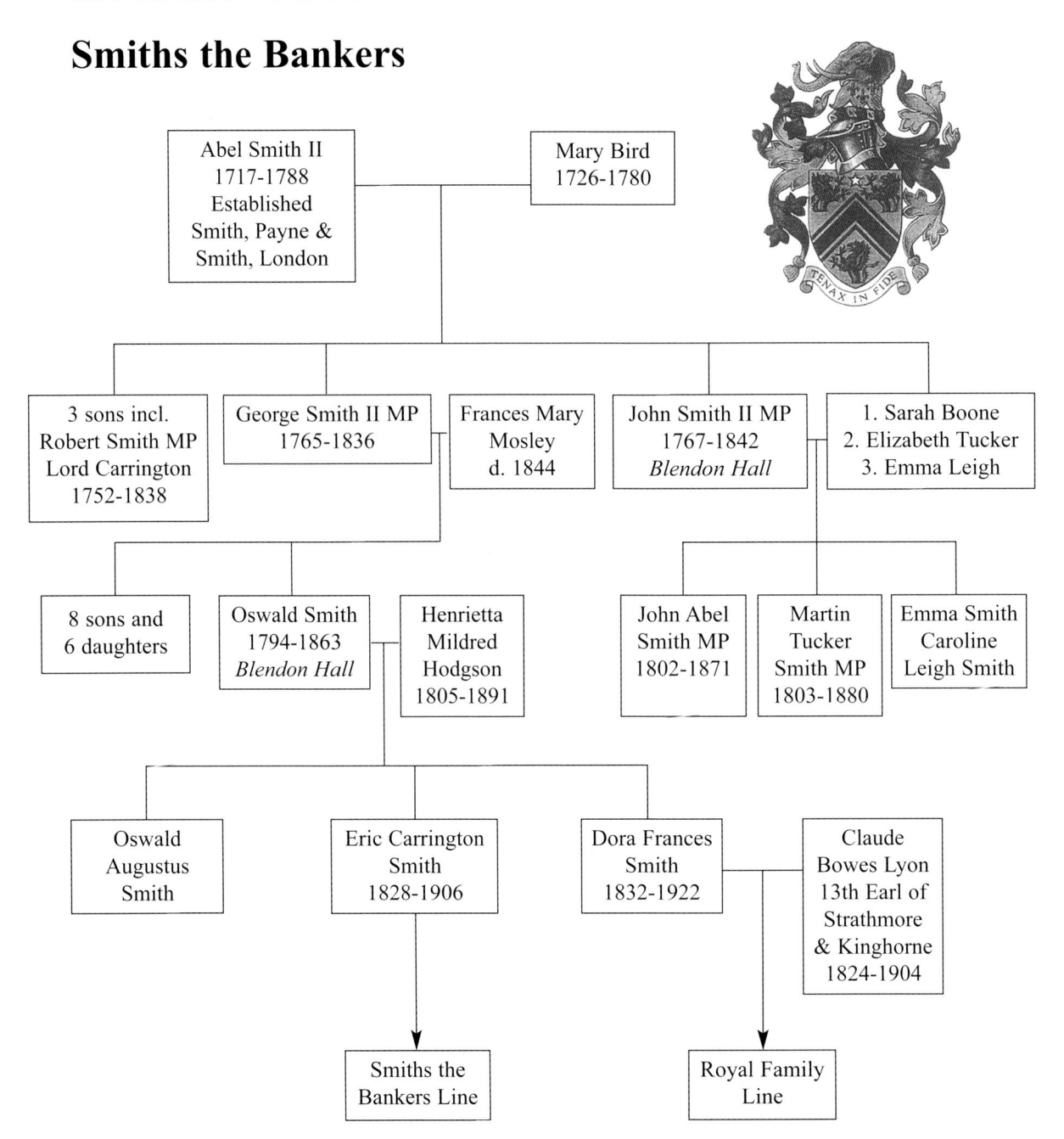

```
Abel Smith II 1717-1788 Established Smith, Payne & Smith, London — Mary Bird 1726-1780
```

Children:
- 3 sons incl. Robert Smith MP Lord Carrington 1752-1838 → 8 sons and 6 daughters
- George Smith II MP 1765-1836 — Frances Mary Mosley d. 1844
  - Oswald Smith 1794-1863 *Blendon Hall* — Henrietta Mildred Hodgson 1805-1891
    - Oswald Augustus Smith
    - Eric Carrington Smith 1828-1906 → Smiths the Bankers Line
    - Dora Frances Smith 1832-1922 — Claude Bowes Lyon 13th Earl of Strathmore & Kinghorne 1824-1904 → Royal Family Line
- John Smith II MP 1767-1842 *Blendon Hall* — 1. Sarah Boone 2. Elizabeth Tucker 3. Emma Leigh
  - John Abel Smith MP 1802-1871
  - Martin Tucker Smith MP 1803-1880
  - Emma Smith Caroline Leigh Smith

Fig 30. Smiths the Bankers – showing the link with the Royal family through Oswald Smith and Frances Dora Smith of Blendon Hall. Source: Smiths the Bankers JASL Boyce 1958

The Smiths – Part I

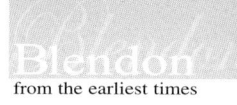

John Smith, like his eldest brother, was a supporter of William Pitt until the latter's death in 1806. It was during his first period in Parliament, in 1804, that Smith became Director of the West India Dock Company. He was to be associated with this company, in different roles, until his late sixties.

Following Pitt's death, Smith supported Grenville's ministry and in the 1806 election he returned to the family's home area of Nottingham. He came second in the poll which meant that he became an MP for Nottingham – holding the seat until 1818.[117]

In November 1806, Grenville asked Lord Carrington, John Smith's eldest brother, whether one of his brothers would second the address at the opening of the new Parliament in December 1806. John was chosen and on December 19th 1806, he paid tribute to the memory of William Pitt. He also, in the same speech, took the opportunity to register his opposition to the slave trade.[118] He would return to this theme throughout his time in Parliament.

In the new Parliament of 1807, Smith followed his brother's line of opposition. It was also at this time that he bought Blendon and became Treasurer of the Board of Agriculture – a position that would cause some conflict later in his life when he voted against altering the Corn Laws at his constituents' behest. Smith's voting record now shows a pattern of opposition to the war – based both on cost and the distress such expenditure was causing to the poor. He also demonstrated sympathy for the plight of working people as a whole. He opposed the Copenhagen expedition in 1808 and supported Whitbread's bid for peace – believing that the state of Ireland demanded an end to hostilities. In the same year he approved the local militia bill, as it was a volunteer arrangement.

In his personal life, Smith suffered another blow. His wife Elizabeth died in April 1809 aged 35.[119] It would be another two years before he married, for a third time, to Emma Leigh, daughter of Egerton Leigh of West Hall, High Leigh, Cheshire and she bore him two daughters.[120] It was also in 1811 that the three Roman urns with human remains were found on the Blendon Hall Estate.[121] In the same year Smith became deputy chairman of the West India Dock Company and then in 1814, chairman. In 1813 he also became a Director of the Imperial Insurance Company.[122]

Throughout the Parliament from 1812 to 1818, Smith continued with his opposition to the war and used a number of opportunities to highlight the distress in the country. Specifically, he supported the abandoning of the death penalty for machine breaking – believing transportation to be more practical – the death penalty being difficult to impose. He also, during this period, opposed

The Smiths – Part I

the rate burden created by the building of the new Kent gaol at Maidstone and the closure of the prison at Dartford – which was close to Blendon and therefore meant that any local trouble could be dealt with more easily.[123] It was also at this time that Smith turned his attention to changing Blendon. The Hall was now about fifty years old and he decided on some improvements.

Smith turned to John Shaw, a Bexley born architect and surveyor.[124] Shaw was related to the Lathams who were the recipients of tithe payments in Bexley (see Chapter 8). Shaw had already done some alterations for John Malcolm at nearby Lamorbey Park. Shaw was to become the architect and surveyor of Christ's Hospital in London, to which he made additions totalling about £30,000. He subsequently became architect to the trustees of Ramsgate Harbour, where he designed the clockhouse and obelisk to commemorate the visit of George IV in 1821. At the same time as he was working on Blendon Hall, he constructed the 'Jacob's Ladder' steps at Ramsgate. Shaw was known for his Gothic designs and this was the approach he took at Blendon. His plans were exhibited at the Royal Academy in 1815 and the result is the design of the building that we can see in early twentieth century photographs. The principal change visible from the outside was the replacement of the large pitched roof to the crenellated Gothic roof. Details of the internal modifications, if any, have not survived. The 'Gothic style' was not universally admired. Byron, in 'Don Juan', heavily satirised Gothic changes. The reader can judge for him or herself as to whether the original or Gothic design is more attractive to the eye. A housemaid records a view from the inside of the property in the early twentieth century as to how she saw the Hall (See WEA extract, Chapter 10).[125]

Interestingly, Shaw and his son were also pioneers in the development of the concept of suburbs of semi-detached houses set in irregularly aligned roads rather than of terraced houses in grids of streets.[126] What would he have made of the Blendon estate as developed by D C Bowyer? But Smith had not finished yet. Having got Shaw to re-design the Hall, he turned to Humphrey Repton to re-design the grounds. Repton was, by 1816, at the end of a very prominent and successful career of landscape gardening. Repton created 'Red Books' showing the before and after of his designs on estates on which he worked. Sadly, it appears that no 'red book' remains for Blendon but there is a fragment that has survived with two prints showing the before and after as conceived for the Hall and landscape of Blendon.

The fragment is reproduced over in full.[127] It tells us a lot about the estate – and also raises further intriguing questions.

Blendon
from the earliest times

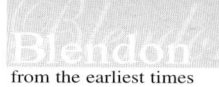

The Smiths – Part I

Fig 31. Print of the Hall before the proposed Repton changes.

Fig 32. Print of the Hall after the proposed Repton changes. The conservatory was not added until some time later and there is no evidence that it was ever crenellated

The Smiths – Part I

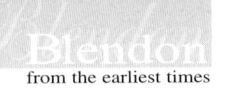

Fragment on Blendon Hall Kent, A Villa belonging to John Smith Esq., MP

From the relative position of this place with respect to the capital, it must be treated as a villa, rather than a constant residence. This distinction is necessary to explain the principle of its improvement, because in the art of landscape gardening two things are often confounded, which require to be kept perfectly distinct, viz the landscape and the garden. To the former belong the lawns, the woods, the water and the prospect; these may be improved by imitating nature but a garden, as I have often repeated is a work of art. At Blenden Hall the lawn is beautiful in shape and its surface enriched with venerable trees which are sufficiently numerous without the aid of firs and Lombardy poplars; and the boundaries are generally well concealed, or blended with distant woods.

The water at present consists of two distinct pools; these may be united in appearance without altering the levels which would sacrifice too many good trees, if the lower water were raised, and make the banks too steep if the upper water were sunk. A bridge however may be so constructed as to give continuity to the water, making it resemble a river: and this idea would also be assisted by extending the water to the east, as marked on the ground. With such alterations the water will become a very important feature in the scenery, which, without it, would require some more distant views beyond the place; but a river is always sufficient itself to form the leading feature of a natural landscape; and with such interesting objects of lawn, wood, and water, in the home scenery, the distant prospect may be dispensed with.

It has been suggested that the approach from Eltham ought to be removed to the corner of the premises, in conformity with a commonly received practice in Landscape Gardening but I prefer the current entrance for the following reasons: I seldom advise entering at the corner of the premises, and in this case the house would present itself almost immediately; a road would cut up the lawn, and oblige us to continue the water, as a river, along the whole valley, which is not otherwise advisable, because there are no rooms in this front of the house to require such waste of lawn and expenditure. Perhaps the fence ought to be kept very low at the corner, to give the public a view into the lawn, which would increase the importance of the place more than by leading a road through it. And lastly the cottage is well placed to act as a lodge, and may be easily ornamented for that purpose.

The entrance may serve as an example for a general remark, which will frequently be applicable to other places. The Gate at present being in the

The Smiths – Part I

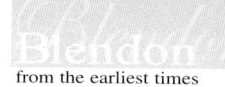

continued line of the paling, there is hardly room to enter commodiously. If the Gate be set back a few yards, the trees, thrown out into the road, will give that degree of importance to the place which we may believe belongs to the manorial right, while a pale, enclosing every tree and bush near the road, counteracts this impression. One other general remark may be useful, however trifling, viz although the interior fences (to be less visible) may be dark green, yet the entrance gate and its immediately attached fence, should be white, a little subdued, to avoid the offensive glare of paper whiteness, yet sufficiently white to prevent accidents which an invisible gate is apt to occasion after sunset.

The House

The House having adopted a new character, from its late alterations, I have subjoined a sketch of its south and east fronts, to explain the effect combined in perspective, which may serve of removing some tall trees, by which it is now oppressed, and deprived of that consequence which its Gothic character has assumed. This sort of comparative influence of trees on a building deserves attention; and the sketch presents a favourable specimen of that species of Architecture, which has already been mentioned as Wyatt's Gothic, because introduced by that Ingenious Architect; although not strictly in conformity with the Abbey, Castle, or Collegiate characters, or even with that of the old Manor-house; but since it evidently belongs rather to the Gothic than the Grecian style, it will be advisable to adopt such expedients as best assimilate with buildings of the date of Queen Elizabeth, all which relate to the appendages; especially as they add not only to the comfort, but to the picturesque effect of the mansion; among these may be reckoned the forecourt, which extends a degree of neatness a little farther into the lawn, and this being fenced by a dwarf-wall, should be entered by a gate in the centre.

There is an old building at the south west corner of the house, which may form the back wall of a conservatory and a similar wall may form a correspondent wing at the north west corner but if this were left open, it would rob the house of its importance, the pleasure ground of its privacy and the character of the place take no benefit of the Gothic style; because such walls add greatly to the shelter in the winter; and there are many plants, such as jasmine, and creepers requiring the support of a wall, which so clothed, forms a luxuriant decoration to a garden in summer and by ivy and other evergreens may partly be extended through the year. This naturally leads to the consideration of the Gardens, and their improvement. Under this head must be included every part of the grounds, in

The Smiths – Part I

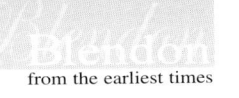

which Art rather than Nature is to please the eye, the smell, and the taste. Each part will require fences, and perhaps of various kinds. First, near the House, a walled Terrace, to keep cattle from the windows, and protect a border of flowering plants near the eye. Secondly an iron Fence may be sufficient to exclude cattle from the pleasure ground; but in that part which contains fruit, a more substantial guard against man must be provided, and brick walls are the best security.

I will here make some remarks on the occupation of land belonging to a Villa. It is surprising how tenacious every gentleman is of grass land, and with what reluctance he increases his garden, or contracts his farm; as if land were only given to produce hay, or to fatten cattle. He forgets the difference in value betwixt an acre of pasture and an acre of fruit garden; or the quantity of surface required to grow a load of hay or a load of currants, cauliflowers, or asparagus, with the value of each. For this reason, the prodigious difference in Gardens of a Villa should be the principal object of attention and at Blenden Hall, the ground betwixt the fruit-trees in the orchard, which produces hay, small in quantity and bad in quality, might be turned to more advantage by planting currant bushes, or sowing garden crops; which even if sent to market, will yield five times the value of the feed for cattle. There is a clipt quickset-hedge,

Fig 33. Humphrey Repton
(Reproduced by kind permission of www.gardenvisit.com)

The Smiths – Part I

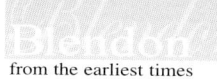

which forms the south boundary of the garden; this is as secure as a wall, and therefore worth preserving. I must also advise retaining the lofty wall to the west, as the greatest protection against the west winds: but a skreen of trees, rather filberts and fruit trees, should be planted, to hide the wall from the approach, and to secure a slip on the outside, and make both sides of this lofty wall productive. If more wall be required, they may be added as described on the map so as to shelter each other from blights, for it is not necessary that the garden should be a square area within four walls. A fruit garden may be so blended with flowers and vegetables, as to be interesting in all seasons; and the delight of a garden highly cultivated, and neatly kept, is amongst the purest pleasures which man can enjoy on earth.

So what are we to make of Repton's critique? What does it tell us about early nineteenth century Blendon?

The first few lines reveal what we can already have surmised from a number of earlier references. Blendon was not a permanent residence for many of its owners or tenants, but a country retreat from London. The Delamottes, for example, had their London home near Fresh Wharf, as would the later Pickersgills and others. There must have been long periods when the 'Master' or 'Mistress' would not be 'in residence' and trusted stewards, whose names have not come down to us except in a few cases, managed the Estate. This is supported by nineteenth century censuses.

In paragraph two, Repton refers to the 'Water' and he is proposing a bridge be constructed and the 'bottom' lake extended eastward. The bridge was certainly constructed – positioned at the foot of the hill of where The Avenue is on today's estate. We can only surmise that the lake was extended (see 1825 map).

In paragraph three, Repton advises against removing the 'approach from Eltham' to the corner of the premises. In the absence of the map – which he alludes to later in the text, this is an intriguing reference. We know that the original entrance to the Estate was from the north, near where Beechway now stands. There are two ways to read Repton's comment:

- That there is already an entrance to the Estate from the north west part of the property, but that it should be re-aligned 'to the corner of the premises' (i.e. the exact north-west = which would put it on the corner of Blendon Road and Penhill Road)

- That the 'present entrance' refers to the Beechway entrance and it is this one that should be 'removed to the corner of the premises'.

The Smiths – Part I

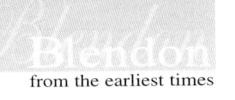

The reader needs to refer to the 1825 map to judge which of these two interpretations is the more likely. In support of the second interpretation is the fact that the 1766 and 1783 maps show no road in the vicinity of the north west of the estate at all. However, the first interpretation is supported by Repton's comments that the Hall would be viewed immediately on entering the Estate. (The alignment, as shown on the map, shows wooded land obscuring the view.) The water (or lack of it) in the valley would also be more quickly apparent if we take the first interpretation to be the correct one. The reference to the 'Cottage' could also be to a building on the site of what became 'West Lodge'. It would seem therefore that Smith has followed Repton's advice and by 1825 the road is shown coming into the Estate where the present Drive comes off Blendon Road.

One also wonders if Repton's safety-first comment in the last paragraph was occasioned by an accident. Perhaps he, or someone he knew well, had come to grief approaching dark painted gates after sunset!

When he turns to the house, Repton refers to 'removing some tall trees' close to the Hall. Repton also suggested the planting of trees – some of which survive to this day – notably to the west of the top lake between The Drive and Cedar Grove and in Beechway.

Repton's recommendations about walls and fences seem also to have been implemented. The 'dwarf-wall' around the forecourt is clearly visible in the photographs of the destruction of the Hall in 1934. His remarks about fences and walls can be seen to have been incorporated from the 1825 map. Some of these iron fences survive to this day, incongruously appearing in back gardens in Beechway, amongst other places, erosion sometimes exposing their top horizontal piece and vertical piles. The 'pleasure grounds' that he refers to is an area of about two acres south and southwest of the House and incorporating the 'top lake'. The fruit gardens – for which Repton recommended 'a more substantial guard against man', are another two acres further to the southwest. The walls that were erected became a conspicuous feature of the Estate and were commented upon by many visitors to the Estate in subsequent years. Footings of these old walls still exist in back gardens in The Drive and are about 15 inches in breadth. Repton also refers to an 'old building in the southwest corner of the House' which may form the back wall of a conservatory – and he had this drawn into the print. However, the 1825 map suggests it was not yet built when Smith moved on. We can however see the 'correspondent wing', on the northwest corner but this was to disappear in later alterations. Sadly, to our knowledge, the map that he refers to has not survived.

The Smiths – Part I

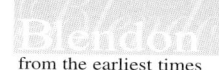

Fig 34. A London Plane tree in Beechway. This tree is over two hundred years old and is possibly one of a number of Repton plantings. Sadly some of the original Repton cedar trees (one is visible in the distance) were lost at about the time of the 'great storm' in 1987.

We now need to return to Smith the Member of Parliament to close this chapter on Blendon's history. Looking again at his voting record we can see that, consistent with his earlier voting, Smith opposed the war against Bonaparte in 1815 – stating that the country could not afford the war, and by 1816 was criticising ministers for their stated belief that the country was flourishing.[128]

In 1816 and 1817, he visited France and lamented that he had to endorse a Frenchman's claim to him that 'all the boast of English freedom was a mockery'.[129]

In 1818, Smith gave up Nottingham and opted for a quiet seat 'on his brother's interest' (i.e. one that he effectively had in his gift) in Midhurst. It is during this time that Smith's philanthropic interests come to the fore and he expresses support for Wilberforce (the anti-slave champion and also Smith's cousin), Elizabeth Fry and a supporter of the regulation of cotton factories. He went to New Lanark in 1819 to see Robert Owen's experiment in social and factory management and told the House about it. During this time, he crusaded against fraudulent bankruptcies, bank note forgeries and abuses in charitable foundations.[130]

The Smiths – Part I

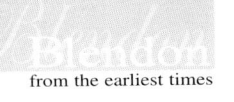

By the end of the decade, Smith's attendance at the House was to become less regular. He remained, however, an MP at Midhurst till 1830, then briefly at Chichester and finally Buckinghamshire – where it had all began thirty years earlier – until 1834.[131] Also in 1834 he officiated at the laying of the foundation stone at the Smith, Payne and Smith building at 1 Lombard Street with the following address:

'I invoke the Almighty Disposer of all events (without whose sanction no human exertion can avail) to look down on this our undertaking, to give permanence to this Building and to maintain the prosperity of the Family connected with it, so long as they shall continue to conduct their affairs with Fidelity, with Industry and with Honour – and no longer.'[132]

Smith retained his interest in the banking firm till the very end of his life and we have correspondence to him about it in his seventies. Sadly, in 1842, he died of accidental poisoning.[133]

Two other items are worthy of note. Smith and his family, owners of Blendon Hall, are 'registered' as users of pews in St. Catherine's Chapel at St. Mary's Church in Bexley (see Pickersgill versus Mee Fuller, Chapter 9 and also Lady Mary Scott in Chapter 5) and Smith is also shown as the owner of The Golden Lion Inn in Bexleyheath. This inn stood facing the entrance of the "Bexley Road", so called because it was the point where travellers bound for Bexley branched off from the highway. The present name of Lion Road arose from the fact that the sign of The Golden Lion used to stand on the triangular piece of land in the middle of the road.[134]

Smith left Blendon in 1824. Why he moved is not clear – it was, after all, only eight years after he had carried out major alterations to the place.

What artefacts come down from Smith's time? This is difficult to answer. It may be that Smith put some of the grander internal fixtures and fittings in at the same time as Shaw was changing the building (e.g. the marble fireplaces) but they may date from Mary Scott's time. Perhaps the early nineteenth century silk wallpaper that featured in the 1929 sales originated from Smith – but possibly the later Pickersgills or Jays bought it themselves.

What we will see within a decade of Smith's departure is a list of all fixtures and fittings at Blendon (see Chapter 7), which gives us an idea for the first time of some of the detail and splendour of Blendon. Some of the remaining iron hurdles that emerge in gardens from time to time probably come from this period. So what we are to make of Smith from a twenty-first century

The Smiths – Part I

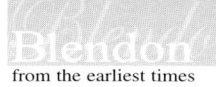

perspective? He was no liberal, as we would define such a person today. He was first and foremost a banker who deplored war from both a financial viewpoint – and also a social perspective. He appeared to show a genuine concern for people's welfare (he consistently opposed slavery) and perhaps demonstrated a greater liberalism later in life than earlier. However we view him, he left his mark on Blendon for all of us to see, touch and admire.

Fig 35. Early nineteenth century Silk Wallpaper. This item was excluded from the 1929 sale of Hall items, although it was featured in the catalogue. This type of wallpaper was suspended on battens so was moveable rather like a tapestry. (Bexley Local Studies)

The Smiths – Part I

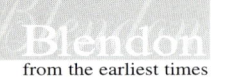

Fig 36. Iron fencing was 'everywhere' on the Estate according to Jim Bowyer. It appears in a number of Blendon photos. Most of it was removed. Some however survived. This section runs incongruously through the back gardens of two adjacent houses in Beechway for over twenty feet appearing, just above the ground. Digging down has revealed the horizontal crosspiece. This section was probably 'buried' and has slowly re-emerged with gentle soil erosion.

Fig 37. Footings of the walled garden in a back garden of a home on the south side of The Drive. The walls were quite thick – about 15" across. The walled garden was a notable feature of the Estate and is referred to in the Garden Life article reproduced in Appendix II

Chapter Seven

Between the Smiths – The Campbell family – 1825–1839

Mrs Mary Lewin, of the neighbouring Hollies, writing to her son, Lieutenant William Lewin in India on May 17, 1826, comments about Blendon: "Our neighbours as you left them except Blendon Hall sold to a Lady Vincent, since dead, but reverting to her daughter, Mrs Campbell."[135]

So it is that we have a belated comment on the sale of Blendon Hall and Estate by John Smith of Grosvenor Square, Middlesex to the Reverend Colin Alexander Campbell in trust for his brother William Johnson Campbell and his wife Anna Maria on September 27/28 1825. [136]

Why Smith chose to move, less than ten years after the Shaw and Repton changes is unclear. He moved to Dale Park in Sussex. Whether, therefore, he wished to be nearer his constituency at nearby Midhurst (which he had held since 1818) or perhaps Campbell's offer and payment for the estate (£15,057 10s 6d) was simply too good to turn down – we do not know. Perhaps his family were growing up and moving on and he no longer required a property the size of Blendon. We do know that by 1825 his eldest son, John Abel Smith (born 1801) was studying for his MA at Christ's College, Cambridge. This John Smith would later join the family-banking firm of Smith, Payne & Smith and also follow his father's footsteps as a Liberal MP sitting for Midhurst and Chichester. Smith's other son, Martin Tucker Smith, also joined the company.[137]

But back to the Campbells and Blendon. Dame Mary Vincent was resident at Debden Hall, in Debden, Essex and her only daughter; Anna Maria had married William Johnson Campbell on 26 July 1817. His younger brother was the Reverend Colin Alexander Campbell of Widdington in Essex.

Who were the Campbells? The family were from Edinburgh and Tofts. John, William's grandfather, was Deputy-Keeper of the Great Seal of Scotland. William's father, Colin, had a distinguished military career in the 71st Regiment joining first as an ensign in 1771 where he saw service in America and promoted major into the 6th regiment in 1783. He married Mary Johnson, eldest daughter of Guy Johnson in New York during this time. Between 1796 and 1810 Colin Campbell was stationed in Ireland. It was here he made his name, putting down rebellion and fighting the French. At the end of his time there, he was major-general in charge of the Limerick district.[138] He was then appointed Lieutenant-Governor of Gibraltar during the most important phase of the Peninsula War and played a critical role in keeping the allied armies in Spain supplied. He died at Gibraltar, in 1814.[139]

Between the Smiths

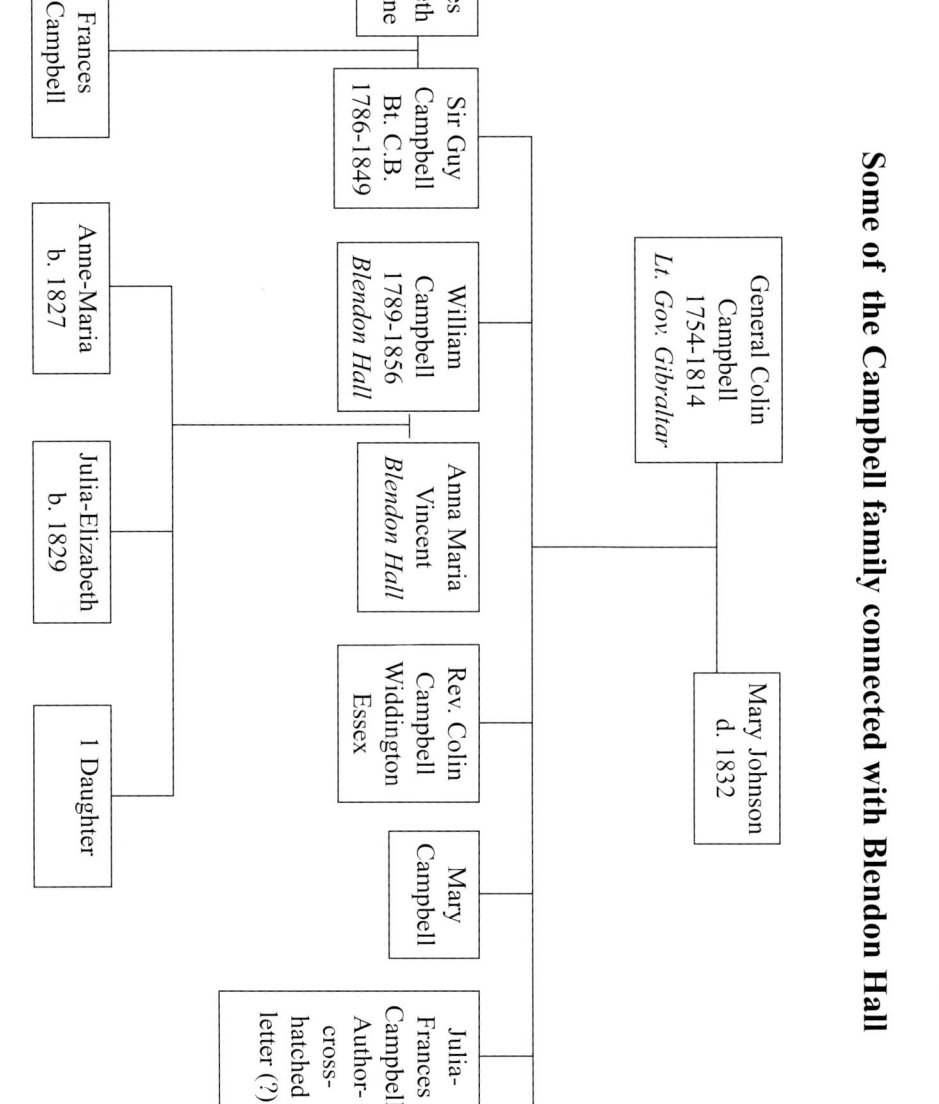

Campbell Family 18th and 19th century
Some of the Campbell family connected with Blendon Hall

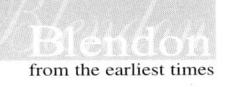

- General Colin Campbell, 1754-1814, Lt. Gov. Gibraltar = Mary Johnson d. 1832
  - Sir Guy Campbell Bt. C.B. 1786-1849 = Frances Elizabeth Burgoyne
    - Frances Campbell
  - William Campbell 1789-1856 *Blendon Hall* = Anna Maria Vincent *Blendon Hall*
    - Anne-Maria b. 1827
    - Julia-Elizabeth b. 1829 — 1 Daughter
  - Rev. Colin Campbell Widdington Essex
    - Mary Campbell
    - Julia-Frances Campbell Author- cross-hatched letter (?)
    - Arabella Campbell

Fig 38.

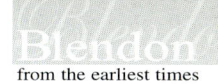

Between the Smiths

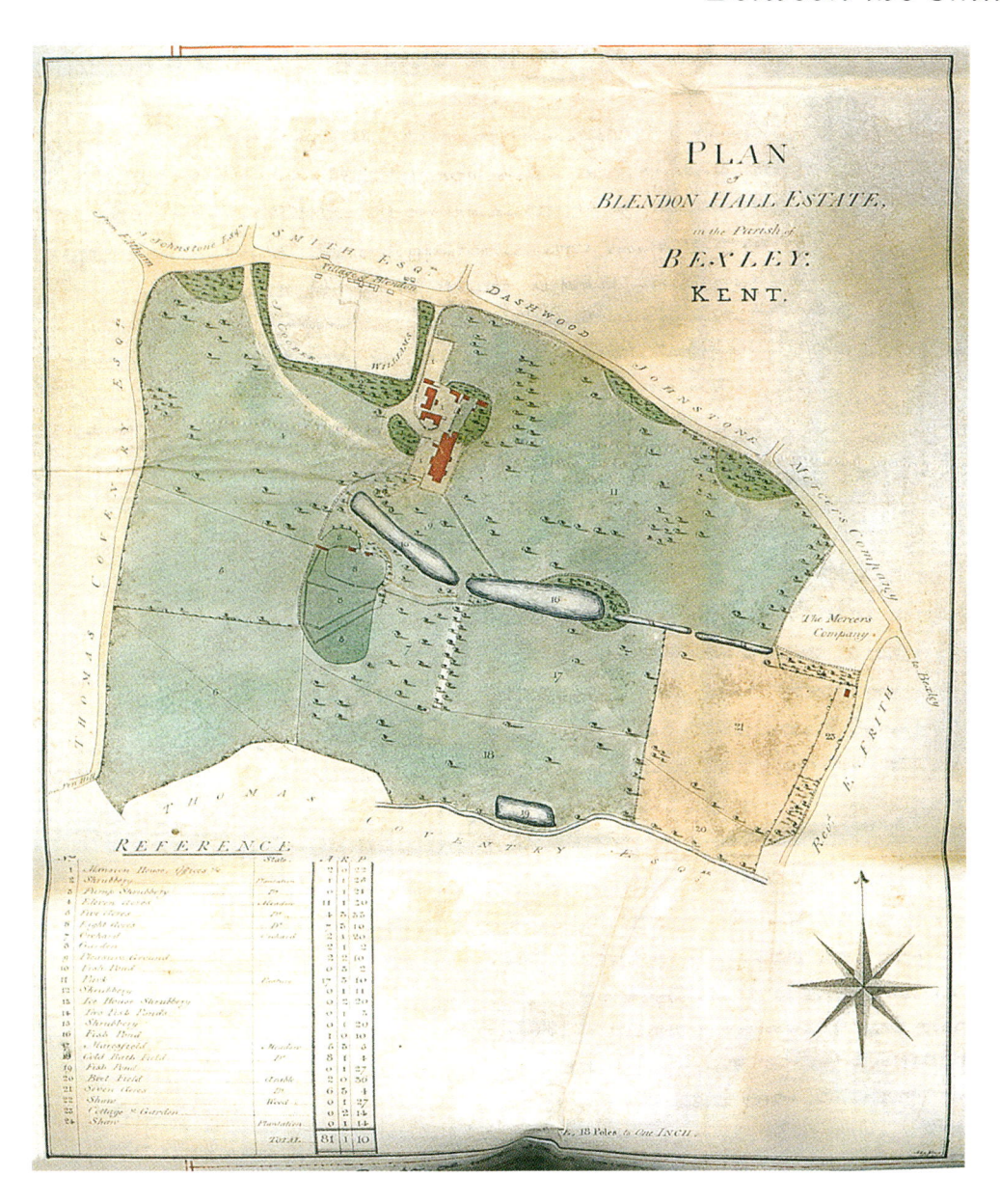

Fig 39. 1825 Map of Estate. The detail on this map is extremely fine and is one of the most visually attractive documents associated with Blendon. (Bexley Local Studies)

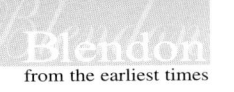

Between the Smiths

His eldest son (William's eldest brother), Sir Guy Campbell C.B., commanded the 6th at Waterloo.[140]

William was one of eleven children[141] – some of whom feature later in this chapter.

Attached to the legal document that records the transaction between Smith and Campbell is a map of the Estate.[142] It is probably the most beautiful extant coloured map of the Hall and Estate. It shows the estate to be a little over eighty-one acres in size and we can see the detail of Repton's changes incorporated in it. Individual trees are depicted – and their shadows are drawn as if the sun is low on the western horizon. The area to the south of Jay's Cottages is shown to be outside the estate (about 4 acres) as is an area on the east of the estate (approximately 3 acres) bounded by Bexley Road and the north of Tanyard Lane.

The Campbells were to remain owners of Blendon for just under fifteen years. In July 1827 they had a daughter, Anna-Maria and in September 1829 another daughter, Julia Elizabeth. At this latter date, William is described as a 'Captain in the army'. Then in the early 1830s we have one of the most fascinating documents to come from Blendon – the crosshatched letter. Its origin is unclear, but it was purchased from a philatelic dealer by Mr Ray Jeal, a local philatelist and postal historian, about 25 years ago. The letter was deciphered in the autumn of 2000 by the Research Service at the Surrey History Centre in Woking,[143] refined by Stella Mayo and is set out below.

Address:
Mrs General Campbell
Belle Ville
Mount Sion
Tunbridge Wells   Blendon
My Dear Mama   5 August

I wrote to Aunty on Saturday and sent my letter by the cross post that you might get it sooner. I was told it would reach you on Sunday, did it?

I must finish now about the Zoological Gardens which are on the same plan as the jardin de plantes, only I think prettier as most of the ground is laid out in flower etc. The habitations of the animals are arranged with great taste. Lord C was as much amused as any of the party and he asked me if Mary would not like a badger for a pet – also another frightful animal - I don't recollect the name now.

Mr. Greathead, who was asked to come with us, did not appear till we had gone half over the garden. I wish he had, for we should have walked more comfortably. As it was, Lord C had to give both arms and you know what that is in a crowd, why very disagreeable, I thought, but he did not mind he is certainly most good-natured. I did not plague him much but Miss B never left his arm once. When Mr. Greathead joined us, he took charge of me as I had left Ld C. I am thus particular - because I know you are apt to understand things different from what they are meant. Mr. Greathead was rather agreeable and seemed charmed with all he saw. We left him in the garden - he is a nice looking young man I think & very good manners. Arabella has bad taste not to admire him.

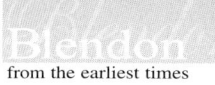

Henry C dined with C but he had not quite recovered from the influenza. None of the children took it. Henry and his lady and baby were here the week I was in town. Mrs. C said she was disappointed at not seeing me as I was her first acquaintance in the Campbell family. They only stayed a few days. The Townshends are coming here on Monday & Miss Scot is expected every day.

Tell Mary that I got the blue stuff - the Palmerine made up in town by Mrs. Giles' mantua maker. It makes it look much prettier now than in the pink. William likes it. I can wear it in the morning or evening as I like. So with the two white gowns I am now very well off. My hair also is getting in to better order. It was all owing to the oil. The bottle, though a stamped label, was counterfeit. The next Arabella gets she better be particular & see if the pattern is laced, no other is genuine. I got it, Arabella will recollect, at Mrs Friends.

As Mrs C & Caroline went to town Tuesday I commissioned Caroline to get me a pink sash - as the one I had with bees was getting rather soiled. She got me a very pretty one & Mrs C bought a feather. She said it matched so well that I must have it. She is good-natured enough & the easiest person to live with, I know of. Also the least attention she is grateful for. I like her upon the whole better than I expected. The children are very dear & all so fond of me I believe they think I must be a child. Aunt Fanny sounds too grave. They call me Fanny, but Mrs C won't have it. She will have every respect paid to elders etc but what I like in them all is that though I play with them they don't take liberties nor make rude remarks.

We all went, William & Maria, also to see the tree which was struck with lightening on Anna Maria's birthday. I told you we had such a storm & we thought it must have fallen somewhere near. In the cornfield, you recollect there are three fine large trees well it is the middle one. You see it from the blue room window - a tree in Lord Bexley's Garden was struck at the same time as a charming cottage where the Miss Townshends live. What is the name? William & Mrs C appeared very little concerned but I said a great deal on the subject to Caroline to make her feel it was a mercy. I wish they felt it as such.

William saw Lord C in town on Wednesday. The carriages weren't the [illegible] to take them to Ditton. They are to come here the 4th week in August for two days - but whether after their visit to Lord Bexley or before, I don't know. My pen is very bad. I have just done, with love to all, your affectionate daughter

Fanny Campbell.

P.s. I have had in all from William 10 pounds that is to say with the 1 pound you gave me. I wrote to Mrs Giles yesterday.

Like so many documents from Blendon, the crosshatched letter raises more questions than it answers. The first question is its date. We only have 'August 5th' on the letter. We can narrow it down to 1829 -1838 on the basis that the Dartford handstamp on the reverse is recorded in use between this time.[144]

Between the Smiths

We can narrow it down further as we know the Campbells gave up the occupancy of the Hall in June 1833 to be succeeded by the Lamberts as tenants. So we are probably reading correspondence from a summer either in the year 1831 or 1832. If the recipient is, as we currently believe, the widow of Colin Campbell (see above) the letter must date from 1831 as she died in May 1832 in Boulogne.[145]

The second question is how the letter reached Tunbridge Wells. Most letters of this era from Bexley went via London – and as a result would carry a postmark showing the year. However, there is a reference to the 'cross post' in the first line of the letter and this explains the route the letter probably took. The 'cross post' involved messengers or couriers setting out from their respective towns (in this case Tunbridge Wells and Dartford/Bexley), meeting half way and exchanging pouches of letters and returning from whence they came.[146]

The next issue is the crosshatched format. This way of writing was adopted because if the letter were written in the normal fashion they would have required another sheet of paper and this would have doubled the postage required from 8 old pence to 1 shilling and four old pence.[147] However, the format is such that to our eyes it is very difficult to interpret. The skill of reading this script is one that we have lost over the years. One of the problems with it is being clear as to where it ends – and where one section fits with another!

Then we need to work out the status of the author – 'Fanny Campbell'. She is writing to her mother 'Mrs General Campbell' who is the widow of General Colin Campbell (see above). We believe the author is therefore Mrs General Campbell's ninth child, Julia-Frances – a younger sister of William.

After this, the rest of our thoughts on the content of the letter become educated guesswork.

The questions and inferences that we can make are as follows:

Paragraph 1

Is her mother staying with Fanny's aunt at Tunbridge Wells for a summer break – and is Fanny similarly on holiday at Blendon?

Paragraph 2

This letter appears to be following another in which Fanny has already described the Zoological Gardens. These had only been open since 1828 and would have been quite a novelty. The reference to the 'Jardin des Plantes' suggests Fanny had been to Paris to see the French equivalent. Is Mary one of Fanny's elder sisters?

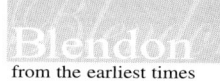

Paragraph 3

The reference to the social problem for a man to have a woman on either arm in a crowd is fascinating! Clearly there is some aside being made both to Fanny's mother and Arabella. Is 'Arabella' Fanny's younger sister? (An 'Arabella' is listed as one of Mrs Campbell's children)

Paragraph 5

A timely warning about counterfeit oil!

Paragraph 6

Are the children William and Anna-Maria's children – Anna-Maria (born 1827) and Julia Elizabeth (born 1829)? Records suggest there is one other daughter as well. Is this 'Caroline' – or is this Caroline the same one as mentioned in paragraph 7 and therefore Caroline Townshend?

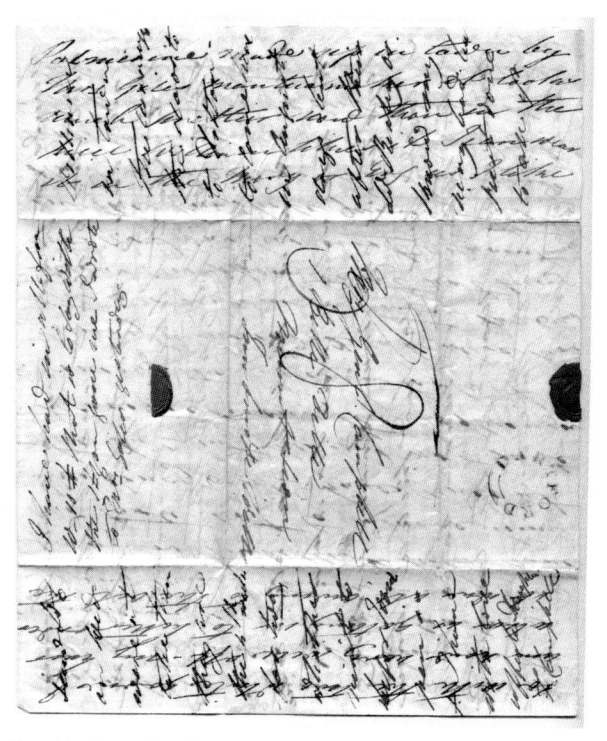

Fig 40. Cross-hatched format. This format is very difficult to read to our unskilled eyes. One of the major problems is where each sections starts!

Paragraph 7

Anna-Maria's christening is July 28th so the date of the lightning incident must be a few days before this.

"The blue room" – one of the first floor bedrooms at Blendon. It was positioned above the dining room on the more northerly bow on the eastern side or back of the Hall.

Lord Bexley is Nicholas Vansittart who lived at Foots Cray Place from c1822 until his death in 1850. He acquired North Cray Place in 1833 including land at neighbouring Tanyard Farm.

The Miss Townshends – a prominent surname in Bexley history – were related to Viscount Sidney, owner of Frognal on the borders of Sidcup and Chislehurst

Between the Smiths

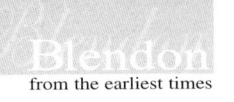

who gave his name to the Australian city. Who is Lord C? Presumably he is the same man that accompanied Fanny to the Zoological Gardens. Is he Lord Camden who lived in Chislehurst?[148] Who is Mrs Giles? Is she the prominent landowner at Blendon?[149]

So there it is. A short social exchange about one hundred and seventy years ago. If only we had a reply or further contextual information. What happened to Fanny is also a mystery. If we have correctly identified her as the author we have contradictory documentary evidence as to whether she or one of her sisters (Arabella) married in 1836 Rev William Henry Tudor MA of Trinity College Cambridge. The Gentleman's Magazine 1836 states: "26th July 1836 at St Martins Church the Rev William Henry Tudor of Trinity College Cambridge to Julia Arabella Maria fourth daughter of late Lt. Gen. Campbell Lt. Gov. of Gibraltar." Debretts Baronetage however, states that it was Julia Frances who married Tudor!

Within one, perhaps two or at the most three years the Campbells have decided to rent Blendon to Mr Charles Lambert. Perhaps William's army commitments involved travel overseas. In 1840 he is in the Pyrenees (See Chapter 8). William is recorded as dying in Nice in the 1850s in the Consular deaths.

The indenture that records the agreement between Campbell and Lambert, dated 19 March 1834, is the most comprehensive description of the Hall and Estate to come down to us until the Jay's time.

The seven-year tenancy that is agreed is backdated to 5 June 1833 and is recorded as between Mr William Johnson Campbell and Anna Maria his wife of Mount Street, Berkeley Square and Charles Lambert of Fitzroy Street. The indenture mentions the various parcels of land that made up the estate 'about 80 acres' and agrees a seven year tenancy for a yearly rent of £498 8s 0d which is to be paid at quarterly intervals viz 29th September, 25th December, 25th March and 24th June. Allowance is made to the lessee (Lambert) to collect the hay harvest at the end of his tenancy in 1840.[150]

However, it is the schedule attached to the indenture that is revealing and gives us an insight into the wealth and status of Blendon. In total it lists over sixty rooms, areas etc. and describes the fixtures and fittings in each. It starts at the top of the house and goes throughout the whole estate listing locks, fences, chimneypieces, fixed ladders, and windows – cracked or sound!

Let us start with the **Upper Storey.** This was traditionally the servants' area and so it was at Blendon. Twelve rooms are detailed in total. A typical room description is as follows:

Between the Smiths

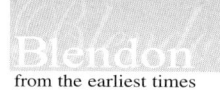

"**No 1 South Room,** or first room from continuation of best stairs – A 21 inch cottage grate with spiked top bar and stone contractions. A deal panelled Chimney Board to fit. A pull, clanks and wires to the bell, line and king wood handle. A patent sash fastening. Two shutter knobs. A spring shutter bar. Two iron rim locks, two keys and brass knobs to room door."

The rooms are predominantly bedrooms, closets and bon rooms (cleaning/linen rooms?). Perhaps the most interesting is **Item 12 – Passages** that has "…Six Bells with spring carriages pendulums and one Nameplate. A ten step painted ladder. A Trap Door and two bolts. A Thumb latch and bolt to Door to Leads. A copper fixed in brickwork and Stove with Iron furnace and doors to supply the Bath with Hot Water. 2 Gilt Copper Ornamental Vanes on the 2 cupolas of Mansion. A brass knob catch to Division Door …"

The vanes and cupolas are presumably Shaw's work in altering the Hall and are clearly visible in later photographs.

The Principal Chamber Storey

This was the first floor and is where the best bedrooms are located – for family and guests. There are 13 items on this floor. One of the noticeable differences from the floor above is the fact that the grates – and presumably the fires – are bigger (37" Rumford grates are specified on this floor compared to 21" or Cottage or 24" Rumford Grates in the upper floor). It is possible that the Lidington Fireplace (see Chapter 9) comes from this storey.

Whilst no measurements are given in his document, it can be used, in conjunction with later ones, to get a broad idea of the layout of this floor – in the absence of an extant floor plan. We are probably looking at some sizeable rooms here and as at other Halls and Mansions, they are distinguished by colour. So we have a Pink, Green and Blue Room. The last one is the room from which Fanny Campbell had viewed the lightning – struck fallen tree a year or two before. It is described thus: **"No 19 Bow Room or Blue Room** adjoining. A 21-inch Cottage grate with spiked top bar and stone contractions fixed. 3 patent sash fastenings. 6 Wood Bars fixed outside, Glass in Window sound, 3 iron shutter bars and 3 spring catches, 6 Walnut Tree knobs and roses, 2 pulls, cranks and wires to the bells. 3 Mortice locks 3 keys and walnut tree knobs to the 3 doors (1 bolt knob deficient)". So we know that Fanny viewed the changed scene through clear, sound glass – or maybe as it was a hot summer, the window was open!

One other 'room' of interest on this floor is **No 25 – Gallery and Best Stairs –** and the interesting comment 'One large square in skylight over Back Stairs

Between the Smiths

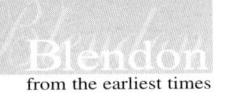

cracked.' – that tells us about pre-Victorian lighting. We can see this skylight in the aerial photo opposite the Preface. **The Ground Floor**: There are eight items here (No 26 to No 33) and it is here we read of the grandeur of Blendon. The rooms are listed as follows – **26 - West Parlour or Spare Bed Chamber** (later to be the Billiard Room); **27 – South Library; 28 – Bow Library** (later to be the Music Room); **29 – Drawing Room; 30 – Dining Room; 31 – Dressing Room adjoining the Hall; 32 – Entrance Hall; 33 – Vestibule and Passage to Pleasure Grounds** (we believe this to later become the conservatory). Traditionally the best room in the house would be the **Drawing Room** and it is described thus: "A handsome statuary marble chimney with Broad shelf decorated with carved trusses and pateras in perfect condition. A veined marble hearth slab, two lever pulls with four ivory knobs cranks and wires to the bells. Ten brass knobs bolts to the French Casements. Three catches with ivory knobs and roses on Shutters. Three long iron bars and spring catches. Three long mitre bars and hooks for ditto. Three squares of plate glass cracked. A mortice lock. Four large ivory knobs and roses and two brass bolts on folding doors. 2 mortice locks. 2 keys & 6 ivory knobs and roses on the 2 small doors." The folding door connecting to the other rooms would give a total length of over 75 feet – plenty big enough for a grand ball! Other items to mention on the ground floor are as follows: In the **South Library** "Those of the Upper Compartments filled with sham books handsomely bound.." and the same is described in the **Bow Library** (later to become the Music Room). One hundred years later Jim Bowyer would remark on these 'sham books' when he and his young teenage friends played and slept overnight in the then empty, and soon to be demolished, Hall.

Domestic Rooms: There are twenty items here ranging from the Butler's Room to Cellars to Larders to Wash House.

The cellars – which feature in subsequent detailed descriptions, are worthy of mention:

No 36 – Cellars: 1st Cellar front Large wood cover to front entrance, 1 small square broken in light over ditto. 5 Guard bars and Iron wire to Door. 2 Painted Trellis pannels to enclose front of ditto. 12 iron hooks in roof. A long dresser on strong legs fixed on one side 12 feet 9 long. A round Iron Grating to drain. A large stove with furnaces and flues to heat the house enclosed by 4 strong Iron doors in perfect Order. The Brick enclosure with Partition for wire fixed on right of Stove, 2 strong shelves fixed over Ditto one with return and wood division under one. An Iron lattice light and wood Cover, 4 Brick Catacombs in small end Cellar. 4 Shelves in Ditto Locks and key to door of ditto. A large strong door to small end Cellar at back. A frame of Iron Guard Bars fixed outside. 1 Squares of Glass in Window cracked. 1 ditto of Lead light ditto,

Between the Smiths

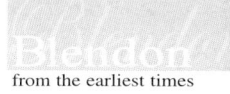

2 Iron Chains 4 feet long fixed in middle Arch. 2 Black Marble Slabs for Chimney 3.3 feet by 1.3 feet. A piece of Portland 2.75 feet by 2 feet. A Frame of strong Guard bars fixed outside of Window of Beer Cellar. Glass in Ditto sound, 2 strong Locks and 2 keys and frame of Six Iron Bars to one. 7 Wood bars to ditto, 21 Catacombs fixed on one side and end of large Wine Cellar, the Brick erection with divisions on both of Ditto . A brick erection with division in ?wall (no door) Large Inner door with Bolt to Cellar Strong Lock and Key to the outer Doors.

We will return to the cellars later.

Other items of note in this section include a reference to a 'Division Door' – a reminder of the very strong social division between family and staff (of which more later). In **40 – The Servants Hall** (which we can see positioned on the 1898 Drainage Map) there is a reference to 'antelope horns' and in **44 – Passage to Offices** there is a 'capital forcing pump' – which supplies 'the upper cisterns'. There is a 'wheel to the large dinner bell fixed on roof wood' and we can imagine the cook turning the wheel to summon the outside and indoor staff to dinner on a warm spring day or a cold winter's day when the frost stayed in the air all day long and your breath could be seen as you spoke. A dog's kennel is also mentioned – there were plenty of dogs at Blendon, as we will see. In Item **49 – The Dairy** – there are "Gothic Windows with crosses" – another reference to John Shaw's work. The last section to consider from this remarkable document is the discrete **areas in the grounds.** There are nine of these and they include the Drying Grounds (where all the washing went to dry – see the photograph opposite the Preface), the Stables, Coach Houses – Stable and Yard, Pleasure Grounds and Kitchen Gardens. In **No 61 – The Pleasure Grounds** we have 'a large leaden cast of a dog on a stone base fixed by the dairy porch' and this item survives to this day. (See Chapters 10 and 11)

Fig 41. Lead cast of dog on a stone base

Between the Smiths

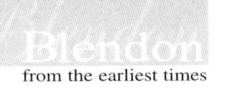

Also in this area we have numerous references to 'iron hurdles' (Repton's recommendation); A reference to the shrubbery near the Ice House on the Bexley Road (opposite where the later built Bridgen School stands) and also to 'young trees' (Repton's plantings?) and a Timber Yard. Iron hurdles were also fixed round the "stump of stone pines"; "thorns"; and "plane trees". There were also '91 three barred iron hurdles fixed round the pond in the flower garden'. We also have reference to Repton's bridge; '8 long iron rods and 18 standards (?) fixed on either side of the bridge, a strong grating and chain to the arch of bridge'. The Avenue also gets a specific mention – there is an entrance gate to it and large iron folding gates. There is also a "sexangular summer house with 3 panelled sides, three Gothic arches and columns in front seat fixed on three sides, thatched roof and ornamental paved floor (the floor and roof in bad condition)." The successor to this summerhouse survives to this day on the estate.

Fig 42. Garden wall. This section was part of the walled garden. Attached to the north side of the wall were plants such as cherry that could thrive in this position. Lead attachments are still in place for holding these plants to the wall.

There are then references to iron hurdles "to keep the cattle from the plantations" (Repton's recommendations) and "the wood erection of bay with drawing sluice" (this is at the eastern end of the bottom lake) "two strong staples, two rings, two chains and pins – a wooden bridge with floor, six Standards, two iron handrails and small gate fixed across the lower piece of water and circular seat with supporters fixed round the elm tree ditto round the lime trees. Metal sundial on circular pedestal … (the shade deficient)". Lastly we have **No 62 – the Kitchen Garden.** Here we have hothouses, thermometers, and flues, trellis coverings, (to walk on), wire for training vines, and references to cucumbers, melons and a leaden pump.

This document tells us so much about the Hall and Estate that we could walk around the area using the author's inventory to guide us.

Charles Lambert certainly got a very detailed listing to everything he took over in 1833 and 1834. At the time of writing, we know relatively little about him or

Between the Smiths

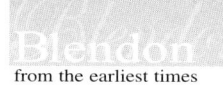

his family. We know he was married to Louise Elizabeth and they had a number of children. One of who was Harriet baptised on 2nd February 1804 at St. Pancras Old Church and we have a letter from her – this time in ordinary script and dated – to her fiancé, John C Smith. It reads as follows:

> My dearest John
>
> As we are not to meet again till Sunday, I cannot allow so many days to elapse without sending you a few lines to enquire after your troublesome cough fearing you may have increased it on Wednesday evening. I did not see any of your family yesterday to learn how you left them but I trust on Sunday you will be able to tell them it is better. We are not expecting any friends down tomorrow, therefore we shall still be alone on the following day, but we must not, I am afraid, anticipate many more such quiet Sabbaths, for I expect shortly we shall assemble a large party. Sincerely trusting this letter will find you better, I remain, as ever, my dearest John.
>
> Yours truly attached
>
> Harriet Lambert
> Friday morning
> November 27th

The issues that this letter raises are as follows:

The letter is stamped 27th November 1835.

This letter was carried by the London Post, which had been extended to the country area in November 1833. Letters such as these could be handed in at Bexley where they received the framed 'T.P. Bexley' handstamp (T.P. - Twopenny Post) – the London Twopenny Post being a development of the London Penny Post.[151] The letter is addressed to J. C. Smith Esq. This J. C. Smith is very possibly related to the former owner John Smith and the next owner, Oswald Smith. He appears to be working in the financial world. (Change Alley in the City) and therefore could be part of the family banking firm of Smith, Payne and Smith. And if 'Change Alley' sounds familiar, it is of course where Jacob Sawbridge plied his more nefarious trade over one hundred years before (see Chapter 3).

The contents of the letter are touching. Harriet, probably on a cold, possibly damp, November morning, is enquiring about her fiancé's health because of his 'troublesome cough'. A cough in pre-Victorian England could soon turn into something very unpleasant and even life - threatening in pre-antibiotic times. We can picture her, possibly in the Bow Library or Drawing Room or perhaps upstairs in one of the grand bedrooms, carefully penning her letter, sealing it, and then asking one of the staff to take it to Bexley. The recipient, John, would have paid for the letter. It arrived the same evening at 7 p.m. on November 27th.

Between the Smiths

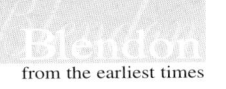

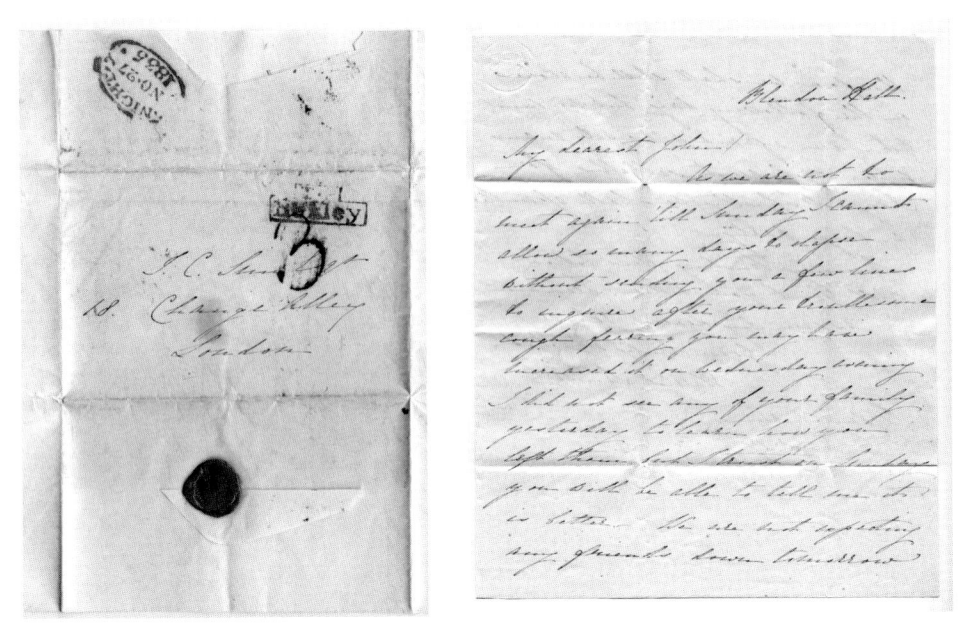

Fig 43. Original 1835 Letter from Harriet Lambert to John Smith.

She also seems to be anticipating a busy period in the run up to Christmas – appropriate socialising was a very important part of life.

Finally, she signs her letter 'Yours truly attached'. We have no record of their marriage in Bexley – perhaps they married in London. Blendon was probably a second home for the Lamberts.

Things, as they say, rarely remain the same for long. And so it was at Blendon. The Blendon Rates tell the story for us. The rates on 8/5/1837 for Blendon Mansion, Ground and Land are shown as £280 with Charles Lambert as tenant and William Campbell as landlord. Then a year later, in the church rates, the entry is for 'the Executor of Charles Lambert'. Sadly, Charles Lambert never collected his hay harvest in 1840 after the formal end of the tenancy. He died in October 1837 and his will is listed in the P.C.C. index – listing his ten children. The will is difficult to read – it appears blurred. In the rates for 9th March 1839 the tenant is 'Smith Esq.' with Campbell as landlord – but the rental value has gone up to £373 6s 8d – Poor Rate having been raised on all properties by a third between May 1837 and March 1839. Was the Smith in this entry Oswald Smith – who certainly later in the year is shown as tenant under his full name or was it temporarily tenanted by John C. Smith – now married to Harriet Lambert? It certainly seems clear that by 1839 Oswald Smith, nephew of the former owner, John Smith was in residence at Blendon.

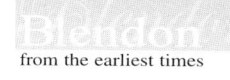

Oswald Smith – Banker and Builder – Part II
The Heyday of the Hall – 1839–1863

Whilst Oswald Smith was in residence as a tenant in 1839, it is on 27/28 July 1840 that we have the documentation of the lease and conveyance of the Hall and Estate from William Johnson Campbell and Anna Maria his wife to Oswald Smith of Lombard Street.[152] (Adjacent to Change Alley – see Chapter 6). We also have a copy of Freshfield and Sons (the solicitor's) detailed invoice for the conveyance of the estate dating between June 8 and September 9 1840. The total invoice is £224 4s and 2d. There is a reference to Campbell being in the Pyrenees (thus delaying completion) and Smith's desire to get on with repairs to the property (the casings were in a poor state) and a court judgement being outstanding against Campbell.[153]

Oswald Smith (7 July 1794 – 18 June 1863) was the nephew of John Smith, the previous owner, but one. He was married in 1824 to Henrietta Mildred Hodgson (1805 – 1891) – daughter of Robert Hodgson, Dean of Carlisle (1766 – 1844) and Mary Tucker (she was the sister of Elizabeth, the second wife of John Smith)[154]. Oswald's father was George Smith of Selsdon (1765 – 1836) fifth son of Abel Smith MP for Nottingham (d.1788).[155] George and John (his younger brother) were in joint control of the London branch of the family-banking firm. George had also been a director of the East India Company and in 1805 was deputy chairman – a powerful and influential role and he used his position in Parliament to defend the company. He apparently turned down a baronetcy because he had fifteen dependants - Oswald being the second of them and he was also a partner in the family-banking firm of Smith, Payne and Smith.[156]

This period, in the mid-nineteenth century, seems to be the heyday of the Hall. Smith changed the Hall and the Estate substantially during this time and the sun appears to shine on him and his family – not least one of his daughters, whose marriage was to impact British history in the subsequent century. Much of his work on the Hall appears to reflect busy social activities with guests coming and going and a general air of wealth and luxury. Clearly, with fourteen siblings and six children of his own a family get together at Blendon was going to be some event!

We do not know why Smith bought Blendon. Perhaps he had happy memories of it as a child when he visited his uncle. He had plenty of opportunities to visit. His mother in law probably visited her sister there as well. Perhaps he

Oswald Smith – Banker and Builder

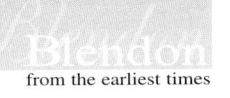

saw the potential that existed which he went on to realise during his time there. Perhaps he saw it as reclaiming a past family home. He was forty-five, forty-six with a young family when he moved in– rich and energetic – it was to be his major project.

The first document to note in this period is the Tithe Map of 1839.[157] The Tithe Map and Assessment was created as a result of the Tithe Commutation Act of 1836, which was produced to regularise payments of tithe to those called 'impropriators' – in Bexley's case the Lathams and Ords.[158] In the listings that accompany the map we have a key stating the discrete number for each area of land, its owner and occupier, name, description and size.

So, for the Blendon Estate, we have four large areas: 1217 – a field of arable covering over eight acres; 1223 – described as 'Coach Road – part of Park' – which is pasture of over fifteen acres; 1232 – Avenue part of Park which is pasture of over twenty-three acres and 1241 – Seventeen Acres which is a meadow of over eighteen acres! There is also reference to four 'ponds' – three in an east-west alignment and one adjacent to the River Shuttle. On the north side of Blendon Road, Oswald Smith owned over six acres including the arable Blendon Field. He is also shown as the occupier of Hoys Field further to the north, which was owned by Anna Johnstone of Danson. Smith also owned a small amount of land at Upton.

We have a photograph of Oswald Smith on a horse, which is undated.[159] This may however be his son – Oswald Augustus Smith. And it is a horse that provides our next, chronological artefact. In the back garden of a Beechway house, sitting equidistant from the house and the boundary fence at the bottom of the garden and from south and north boundary fence is a small memorial stone with the inscription 'To the memory of Karl – October 23rd 1852'. We are reliably informed that Karl was a horse and the estate was well known for its horses (see Chapter 9 and 11 – Warrior the horse). The stone was located near the dairy – close to where the lead dog was also located (see Chapter 7). Jim Bowyer commented that this area was the pet cemetery – where the animals that shared their lives with Blendon estate owners and staff were finally placed and commemorated by small pots of flowers.

In the following year, on September 28 1853, we have the marriage of one of Oswald's daughters, Frances Dora (1832-1922) at Bexley Church to Claude Bowes Lyon (1824-1904) of the 2nd Life Guards. He was the younger brother of Thomas, the 12th Earl of Strathmore. In 1865 he was to succeed his brother to become the 13th Earl. It was this couple who were the paternal grandparents of Elizabeth Bowes Lyon, who became Queen Elizabeth and then Queen

Oswald Smith – Banker and Builder

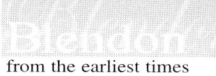

Elizabeth the Queen Mother. Both her grandparents lived long lives – he was over eighty when he died and she was almost ninety when she died in 1922. On the marriage certificate the bridegroom's residence is put down as St. George's, Hanover Square and the bride's as Blendon Hall, Bexley. Her grandfather was Rector of St. George's, so the young man must have stayed there to get the necessary residence qualification. The officiating minister was the Rev. Wilby P. Hodgson, Vicar of Hillingdon, and a relative of Mrs. Oswald Smith. The witnesses were the bride's father and mother, the Earl of Strathmore, Eric Carrington Smith, Oswald A. Smith (her elder brothers) and Henry Dorrien Streatfield.[160] Another of Oswald Smith's daughters, Laura Charlotte, was married when she was nineteen in Bexley Church on April 11, 1848 to Evan Maberley, Captain in the Royal Artillery. She was the great-aunt of Her Majesty the Queen Mother.[161]

Fig 44. Horse Memorial in the back garden of a house of Beechway. The stone is quite small – only about 9" x 12"

Just under a year later, in 1854, in Philip Norman's "Annals of the West Kent Cricket Club" published in 1897, we have recorded details of a cricket match played between Blendon Hall and West Kent Cricket Club.[162] Oswald Augustus Smith, the son of the owner of the same name, was a member of the West Kent Cricket Club and it was he who made the invitation for the match. It appears that the side that he put together was made up of his friends and relations – rather than staff at the Hall. Social divisions clearly were still very strong in the mid-nineteenth century. Of those named, M M Ainslie was Captain of the Eton eleven in 1842, and of the Oxford eleven in 1845. He played quite a lot in the 50's and 60's. He died in 1896. Rev Francis Gosling was the second son of Richard Gosling, the banker, of Woollet Hall, North Cray (now Loring Hall). Other members of the family also played for West Kent. Bowes Lyon had, as previously mentioned, married Oswald's sister and was therefore his brother-in-law. Bowes Lyon's brother, the Earl of Strathmore, is shown, playing at number 3. Other Blendon Hall players included Eric Carrington Smith (Oswald

Oswald Smith – Banker and Builder

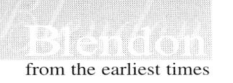

Augustus's younger brother), who was a witness at the previous year's wedding as was a Streatfield (see above). Bowes Lyon scored the highest for Blendon – getting 26 in the second innings, but Blendon crashed to a heavy eight-wicket defeat. I have been asked where at Blendon the match would have been played and I think the probable location is at the back or east of the Hall where the croquet lawn and tennis court were located.

As stated earlier, this was also a period of intense building activity and change on the Estate. In 1855/1856 the two matching lodges were built of Kentish ragstone in a neo-Gothic style to match the Hall. Each building had four rooms and a garden. The West Lodge was located on the corner of the drive up to the Hall (today's The Drive) and this building still stands today. The East Lodge stood at the northern entrance to the Estate (on the north west corner where modern day Beechway meets Blendon Road) and was demolished in the early

At Blendon Hall, August 1, 1854.

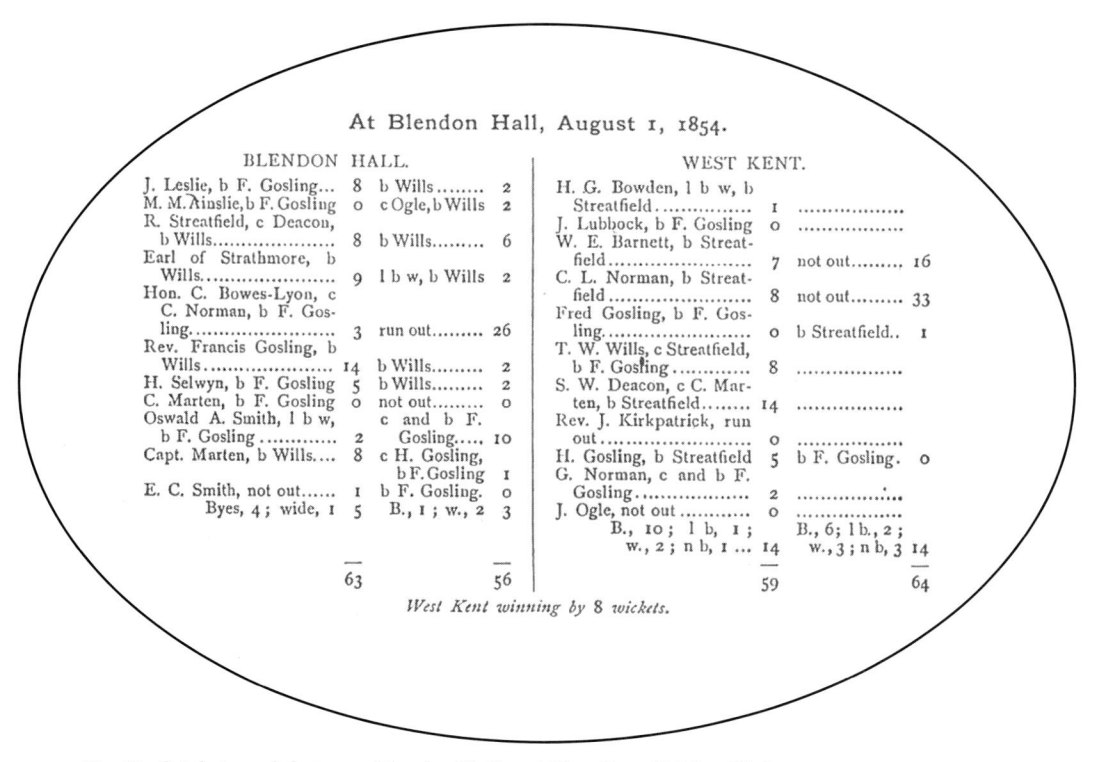

BLENDON HALL.			WEST KENT.			
J. Leslie, b F. Gosling	8	b Wills 2	H. G. Bowden, l b w, b Streatfield	1		
M. M. Ainslie, b F. Gosling	0	c Ogle, b Wills 2	J. Lubbock, b F. Gosling	0		
R. Streatfield, c Deacon, b Wills	8	b Wills 6	W. E. Barnett, b Streatfield	7	not out	16
Earl of Strathmore, b Wills	9	l b w, b Wills 2	C. L. Norman, b Streatfield	8	not out	33
Hon. C. Bowes-Lyon, c C. Norman, b F. Gosling	3	run out 26	Fred Gosling, b F. Gosling	0	b Streatfield	1
Rev. Francis Gosling, b Wills	14	b Wills 2	T. W. Wills, c Streatfield, b F. Gosling	8		
H. Selwyn, b F. Gosling	5	b Wills 2	S. W. Deacon, c C. Marten, b Streatfield	14		
C. Marten, b F. Gosling	0	not out 0	Rev. J. Kirkpatrick, run out	0		
Oswald A. Smith, l b w, b F. Gosling	2	c and b F. Gosling 10	H. Gosling, b Streatfield	5	b F. Gosling	0
Capt. Marten, b Wills	8	c H. Gosling, b F. Gosling 1	G. Norman, c and b F. Gosling	2		
E. C. Smith, not out	1	b F. Gosling 0	J. Ogle, not out	0		
Byes, 4 ; wide, 1	5	B., 1 ; w., 2 3	B., 10 ; l b, 1 ; w., 2 ; n b, 1	14	B., 6 ; l b, 2 ; w., 3 ; n b, 3	14
	63	56		59		64

West Kent winning by 8 wickets.

Fig 45. Cricket result between Blendon Hall and West Kent Cricket Club

Oswald Smith – Banker and Builder

Fig 46. East Lodge – top of Beechway. This photo is taken from today's Beechway looking north towards Blendon Road

1930s. The lodges were home to head gardeners, chauffeurs and other staff during the remaining seventy years of the Hall. A new dairy had also been built with a thatched vaulted roof and opening into a rustic summerhouse at the eastern end.

In 1854 we have the following entry in the D.C. Bowyer Records deposited at Local Studies.[163]

"Conveyance of two messuages and six cottages at Blendon, Mr Frederick Williams and Mrs Louise Giles to Oswald Smith, 28 February 1854"

This change sees the acquisition and integration of the four acres of land fronting Blendon Road and also the properties known as Blendon Villas that were to become Jay's Cottages. Smith clearly had plans for this area because within eighteen months of this transfer the property to the west of Jay's Cottages, which had been rated in July 1855, had been swept away by the time of the next rate in November 1855.[164] Is this reference in the sales transaction to

Oswald Smith – Banker and Builder

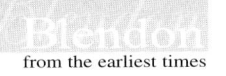

Fig 47. Jay's Cottages have stood in Blendon Road since the early eighteenth century
(Bexley Local Studies)

the same Mrs Giles referred to in the cross hatched letter?

In November 1858 we have a record of a 'Deed of Gift' by Mary Hodgson (Smith's mother in law) of Blendon Cottage to Oswald Smith. In gratitude for his allowing her to live at Blendon Cottage 'without payment of rent or other pecuniary return' she gives to him her 'household goods, furniture and fixtures' at Blendon Cottage (but not including books, pictures, plate, linen and china) on her death.[165] She died coincidentally in the same year as Smith (1863) aged 83.[166]

The next building of note that was created by Smith is the Bailiff's House. On the 1839 Tithe Map, there is a small, unusually shaped piece of land south of the kitchen gardens, which is described as shrubbery or wood. It only occupies 12 perches (a perch is a measure of land equal to $\frac{1}{60}$ of an acre). By the time of the 1860 OS Map the site of the property is more accurately defined and in the

Oswald Smith – Banker and Builder

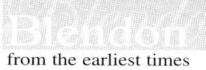

rate book for October 1860 a rate of 17s was paid for a house and garden occupied by a Mr Hills. This could be the Bailiffs House – newly built between the OS Surveyors visit and that of the Bexley Rate Collector. Certainly by 1863 we have the following description:

"The Bailiffs Residence – Is situate in the Park and contains FOUR ROOMS, Scullery, Pantry, Water closet etc with GARDEN, also a Yard with Outbuildings."[167] The garden and area around the Bailiff's Cottage has yielded quite a few artefacts. Apart from the coin mentioned in Chapter 3 from the eighteenth century we have some nineteenth century remains including a grab (possibly for picking up litter or anything out of reach), a horseshoe from a riding or carriage horse, an iron ring with an octagonal inner edge and a raised flange which might be part of a ring spanner or a water valve turner and a window glass pane.[168]

Fig 48. The Bailiffs Cottage in 1929 as depicted in the Sales Catalogue. This was the home of Mr Peter McGready and his wife (see Chapter 11) and the track in front of the cottage runs up to the drive that led to the Hall from the West Lodge. (Bexley Local Studies)

Oswald Smith – Banker and Builder

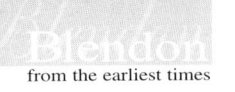

Fig 49. The Bailiffs Cottage today. Extended and modernised a very attractive dwelling in the heart of the Estate.

Smith also developed the Kitchen Gardens and built an orchid house with a peachery and mushroom house. (The peaches produced in this part of the estate are still remembered for their exquisite taste by some of the present and former residents.) In the area that was adjacent to Jay's Cottages and their gardens, Smith had created a wilderness walks area in which he had constructed an icehouse, rustic summerhouse etc. as well as a fernery on the eastern side of the adjacent meadow.

Less clear is the timing for the erection of the Bath House on the southern edge of the estate adjacent to the River Shuttle. In the 1825 map the Fishpond on which it was sited is clearly shown. However in the 1863 inventory of sale it is mentioned. A bathhouse was a spa for taking the waters and is similar to one that survives at 112 North Cray Road. Today, this building would be located south of Bladindon Drive, east of the junction with The Avenue where the road dips down.

Oswald Smith – Banker and Builder

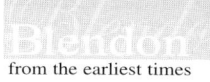

Inside the Hall, Smith had also been busy. He had developed the top of the building to create three bedrooms for servants and on the second floor the two bedrooms in the bows at the back of the Hall have been substantially improved to become: "two lofty bow Bedrooms with arched ceilings" and the whole impression is that this floor has been 'converted' to accommodate guests rather than having the status of the servants' floor.[169]

On the first floor there appears to be a consolidation of rooms – less than before but probably each room on a grander and more luxurious scale. On the ground floor, Smith converted the Bow Library to a Music Room, the West Parlour or Spare Bed Chamber into a 'capital Billiard Room' and developed the 'DELIGHTFUL CONSERVATORY' into a single story room 43'6" by 19'6".[170]

Fig 50. Blendon Cottage. This building stood outside the northeast boundary of the Estate. During the Second World War it was used as a food office. It was demolished in 1954. There are many photos of this building at Local Studies. (Bexley Local Studies)

Oswald Smith – Banker and Builder

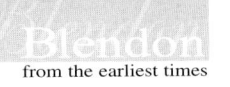

On his death in 1863 a memorial tablet to his memory in St Mary's referred to him as 'a constant and humble worshipper in this church for twenty – five years'.[171] His widow, Henrietta, survived him for many years afterwards.[172] Oswald Augustus Smith (his eldest son) purchased Hammerwood House and Estate in Sussex, which totalled 1700 acres of woodland and farmland. He also provided gas installation and roof insulation at the property as well as being a local philanthropist being the mainspring and chief benefactor of the Victoria Memorial Hospital in East Grinstead.

How can we summarise Oswald Smith's time at the Hall? He clearly loved the place, entertained extravagantly and invested huge amounts of money into it. On his death, a beautiful property came on to the market.

We have one artefact retrieved from a garden that probably dates from this time, which is a candlestick holder that was found near the domestic end of the property.

Fig 51. Candlestick Holder – probably nineteenth century. One of the most beautiful finds on the estate – a glass candlestick holder found in the area of the domestic end of the hall.

Chapter Nine

The Americans are coming! – 1863–1929
William Cunliffe Pickersgill and Anna Riggs Jay

In 1863 William Cunliffe Pickersgill bought Blendon Hall for £24,000. Pickersgill, from New York, was a member of Fielden Bros bankers in London.

William Cunliffe Pickersgill (1811 – 1891) was the son and heir of John Pickersgill of Netherne House, Surrey and Tavistock Square, London. He was married in 1835 to Anna Riggs (1811 – 1892). She was the second daughter of George Washington Riggs (1777 – 1864) a well-known banker, merchant and silversmith from Washington DC, USA and grand-daughter of Samuel Riggs (1740 – 1814). His portrait, with sideburns, used to hang in the hall at Blendon. The Riggs family originally went to America from Hampshire, England in the seventeenth century. The Riggs bank was the bank for most of the U.S. Presidents and it financed the Alaska Purchase and the building of the U.S. Capitol building.

William and Anna had two daughters in their early twenties – Sophia Cunliffe and Anna Riggs and a son William, aged 19. There had been another son, John, who had died as a small child in 1848. All the children had been born on Staten Island, New York.

Years later, Anna Riggs would recall that her father, who made periodical business visits to England, was attracted to purchase the Estate by the "inviting rural beauty of Blendon Hall and its pastoral surroundings".[173]

It is interesting to speculate on local opinion with the arrival of Pickersgill and his relatively small family after all the Smiths. America was at this time going through the turmoil of Civil War and one wonders whether Pickersgill had concerns about his family's welfare in the States. How too would the servants, staff and neighbours react to the Americans? They were bankers – like the Smiths – and Blendon was no stranger to the American link – both Delamotte and Whitefield travelled to the Americas in the 1730s, both Desaguliers and Pattison saw service there later in the same century and Brett had connections with Virginia in the seventeenth century. Perhaps it was 'as you were' for most of those working on the estate. We do know that initially the Pickersgills were only resident at Blendon in the summer months.[174] The 1881 National Census (dated Sunday April 3rd) also shows the Pickersgills residing at their London home.[175]

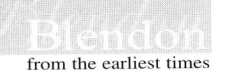

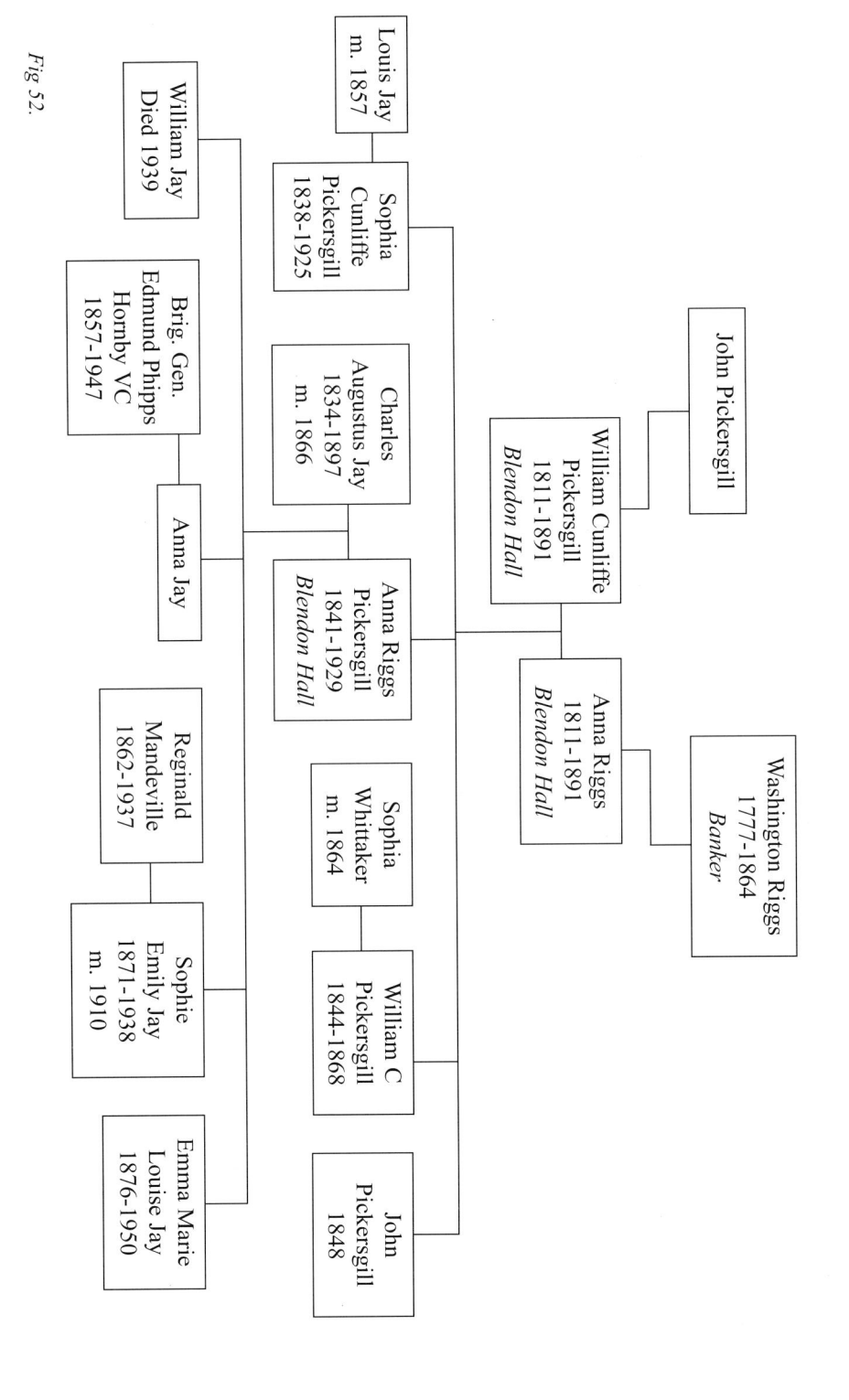

Pickersgill/Riggs/Jay Family – 19th and 20th century

The Americans are coming!

Fig 52.

- John Pickersgill
  - William Cunliffe Pickersgill 1811-1891 *Blendon Hall* (m. Anna Riggs)
- Washington Riggs 1777-1864 *Banker*
  - Anna Riggs 1811-1891 *Blendon Hall*

Children of William Cunliffe Pickersgill & Anna Riggs:

- Sophia Cunliffe Pickersgill 1838-1925 — m. 1857 Louis Jay
  - William Jay Died 1939
  - Anna Jay — Brig. Gen. Edmund Phipps Hornby VC 1857-1947
  - Sophie Emily Jay 1871-1938 m. 1910 — Reginald Mandeville 1862-1937
  - Emma Marie Louise Jay 1876-1950
- Charles Augustus Jay 1834-1897 m. 1866 Anna Riggs Pickersgill 1841-1929 *Blendon Hall*
- Sophia Whittaker m. 1864 — William C Pickersgill 1844-1868
- John Pickersgill 1848

The Americans are coming!

In the year following the purchase of the Estate, Anna Pickersgill's father, George Washington Riggs, died in Baltimore. However, in the same year William, the Pickersgills' son, married Sophia Whitaker in Palermo, Italy.

Then on 7th June 1866 at St. Mary's Church, Bexley, Anna Riggs Pickersgill married Charles Augustus Jay (known as Carl).[176] Jay was born in Frankfurt, Germany, but at the time of the marriage was described as a merchant from New York. The story goes that he and his brother met the Pickersgill sisters on a world cruise and subsequently married them. (Sophia had married the much older Louis Jay in 1857). It was one of Anna Jay's fondest memories that she and her husband travelled, on their honeymoon, in the first train that ran over the Dartford Loop line.[177] Mr and Mrs Jay then moved to 34 Queensgate Gardens, Kensington for the next twenty-five years and brought up their four children.

Within another two years William C Pickersgill junior had died, tragically young at the age of 24. At the beginning of 1869 Pickersgill senior then asked the vicar at St Mary's Bexley whether a tablet could be erected in memory to his infant son, John. The vicar, and churchwardens, respectfully turned his request down on the grounds that the wall is already 'heavily drawn upon by monumental tablets.' and that the 'cutting of the brace…might damage the support of the roof'. They do however suggest a memorial window as an alternative solution. A memorial window of King David with an inscription to John Pickersgill, the infant son who died in 1848 remains in the church to this day.[178]

On more general matters and the changes on the Estate itself we do not have any definite clues as to what Pickersgill did to the Hall and Estate during his time, but there are some indicators. Clearly, he had bought a fine estate, but old houses (Blendon was now a hundred years old) require huge investment – just to maintain and stand still. Comparing the 1863 and 1929 sales documents indicates little change in the last sixty plus years of the Hall. A school - room is mentioned in the 1929

Fig 53. Memorial Window to John Pickersgill at St Mary's Church. (Bexley Local Studies)

The Americans are coming!

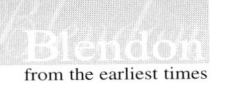

document on the first floor and two nurseries on the second floor – but these may have been relatively late changes to reflect the needs of the Jays' grandchildren.[179] In 1929, lighting is 'by electricity', the 'company's water is laid on' and 'the telephone is installed' – all modern conveniences not there in Smith's time.[180] However we know electricity was not yet installed by 1912.[181]

Pickersgill appointed a new head gardener, a Mr Frederick Moore, in the late 1860s and that Moore stayed at Blendon for over thirty years.[182] In April 1881 the Census tells us that Frederick Moore (aged 40) and his wife Eliza, from Chichester in Sussex, lived at the Bailiff's Cottage and their address is recorded as 'Gardeners House Near Garden in Park Bexley, Kent'.[183]

In the mid 1870s we have a letter to Pickersgill from J M Fuller, the vicar of Bexley, checking with him the rights that he holds as owner of Blendon with regard to certain pews at St Mary's. Fuller is enquiring because there were plans to refurbish the church and he is trying to establish what rights he has in dealing with the interior space. Pickersgill response is robust and swift and he states that the pews have belonged to Blendon for more than one hundred years and he is sure that 'neither you nor the Churchwardens would ask or request me to do any act to alienate them'.[184] By June letters between the two men indicate that the issue has escalated and in effect Pickersgill appears to be saying that he never wants the subject raised again. The whole issue rumbles on with sides being taken and legal advice and support sought. By July 1879 the Commissary Court of Canterbury is judging on the case between Fuller and Layton of Parkhurst, Pickersgill and Dashwood of Hall Place. Whilst Pickersgill fails to establish his prescriptive rights to the pews and therefore the site (following the proposed changes) he does establish his possessory rights to the site.[185]

Fig 54. William Pickersgill's Prayer Book

The Americans are coming!

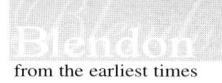

Relationships clearly improve and the tone of letters changes following the court case. In 1883/84 Pickersgill paid £32-16s-7d to the Restoration Committee of St Mary's Church for 20 seats appropriated to "Blendon Hall" – following the long sought general restoration of the Church.[186] The pews still exist in the Church to this day. Interestingly we also have Pickersgill's prayer book extant with his signature inside.

Another item of interest from this period is the 'Lidington' fireplace. The carved oak mantelpiece, which originally had an over mantel as well, was purchased by

Fig 55. – The 'Lidington' Fireplace – still providing a warm hearth today. Note the unusual carvings

Harold Lidington JP in a second hand furniture sale in Woolwich in the 1930's. He was informed it came from Blendon Hall and this is consistent with the fact that many of the fixtures and fittings from Blendon were rescued and sold when the Hall was finally demolished in 1934. There was also a specially designed wrought iron fire basket with it as well. When the property changed hands, the over mantel and fire basket moved on, but the mantelpiece is still in situ. Professional help has been employed in dating and placing the object and the view is that it probably dates from 1865 to 1880 and was purchased from Gerard Street or Wardour Street, Soho. However, the figures on the sides are much older – probably dating from the 1630s or 1640s.[187]

The Americans are coming!

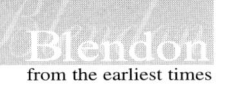

If this was a 'Pickersgill purchase' – which the evidence suggests it was – perhaps it went into one of the posher bedrooms – the major ground floor rooms already had grand marble mantelpieces.

In 1880 William Pickersgill ended a 'tradition' that had existed for over five hundred years at Blendon. Since the mid fourteenth century the owner of the Blendon Estate had paid quit rent to whoever was the Lord of the Manor of Bexley – whether it was the archbishop, the King or Oxford University. The payment excused the landholder from all those services the medieval tenant had to perform for the Lord of the Manor. The quit rent due annually from Pickersgill was £2.17s. 11d. and so in 1880 he paid twenty five times that amount in a lump sum to Oxford University and thereby relieved himself and all future owners of Blendon Estate from having to pay quit rent.[188]

In the 1881 National Census of England and Wales, Pickersgill (for some reason missing the 's' in his name) is recorded, aged 69, born in London living at 58 Prince's Gate, Westminster and being a JP of Kent. Anna his wife is also 69 and recorded as 'not born in the UK'. Sophie C Jay (his daughter) aged 42 and married and her two children – Louis 19, a student and Addie 16 are also recorded as living at Prince's Gate. The assumption is that Sophie's husband, Louis, is abroad.

There is a list of ten servants living with the Pickersgills. William Watkins is the butler, aged 48 and married and originally from London. (The Watkins name is a familiar Bexley one – Tanyard Farm in Tanyard Lane being home to a Watkins family for hundreds of years although there is no obvious connection between the two). One of the two footmen is George Harper aged 28 and single from Middlesex (see Chapter 10).

Meanwhile in Kent.... on the day of the Census we have two staff recorded at the Hall – Mary Ann Baker, 47 a dairymaid and Steven Howell a gardener, 45. We also have Owen Soden and William Saunders – both 20 and domestic servants recorded as '2 Men Sleep in Garden'.[189]

What conclusions can we draw from this? The Pickersgills' large retinue of staff must have travelled with them and decamped with the family when they went from one home to another. There appears to be no housekeeper at Blendon when the family is at Prince's Gate. It is fascinating to find two men 'located' in the garden – presumably overseeing the heating in the greenhouses and gardens.

The Americans are coming!

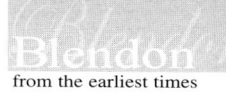

Elsewhere in Blendon we have addresses that are becoming familiar – including The Lodge (2 separate entries), Blendon Cottage, The Public House (presumably 'The Three Blackbirds'), the Cottage opposite Blendon Gates (3 separate entries), Blendon Corner and School (presumably Bridgen School).[190]

A few names are also appearing that become familiar later on in the Blendon story. We have the Lainsheers – with Eliza Lainsheer aged 40 recorded as a laundress (see postcard from the Hall to Hazelwood House later in this chapter), the Cousins at one of the Cottages opposite Blendon Gates (the Cousins were a large Bexley family) and the Johnsons with their growing family at another of the Cottages opposite Blendon Gates. Perhaps the most surprising detail to emerge from these records is the diversity of origin of the various individuals living at Blendon. They came from all over the country.

Our next reference to Pickersgill comes courtesy of a few residents at Blendon, who have, attached to their title deeds, the "abstract of the title to freehold premises in the county of Kent". It is Pickersgill's will, dated 12th July 1890 in which he is described as being resident in Blendon Hall and "of No 77 Marina Street, St Leonards-on-Sea, Sussex". Presumably he had bought a residence by the seaside for relaxation and taking the sea air and perhaps for his health. In the will Pickersgill leaves Blendon Hall and Estate to his wife (for as long as she wishes to reside there) and then to his trustees upon trust for his daughter Anna Riggs Jay and after her death upon trust for such one or more of her children. The trustees are Carl Jay (his son-in-law), John Fielden (of Fielden Bros), Thomas Davison and Theodore Lodge.

In September 1891, Pickersgill adds his other daughter, Sophia Cunliffe Jay to the list of executors and trustees. In November of that year he died. Within a year, Anna Pickersgill died, followed a year later by John Fielden (a trustee) and then tragically in 1897, at the age of 63, Carl Jay – Anna Riggs' husband, who had only recently taken occupancy of

Fig 56. Pickersgill's seaside home, 77 Marine Parade Hastings, today

The Americans are coming!

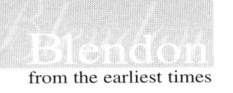

the Hall. The Blendon Hall Estate was still subject to a trust and the trustees were changed in 1897 to include Louis Jay, William Cunliffe Pickersgill Jay (Pickersgill's grandson) and Carl Borgnis, along with Thomas Davison (four in total) – Theodore Lodge and Sophia Jay withdrawing from the trust. By 1902, Thomas Davison had died.

The last tenant of the Hall was Anna J Riggs Jay. She was the youngest daughter of W C Pickersgill and was born in Staten Island, New York on January 31st 1841. Thus when her husband Carl died in 1897, she was only fifty-six. She had four children – William, Anna, Sophie and Emma and because of their close links with Blendon we shall consider each one in turn shortly.

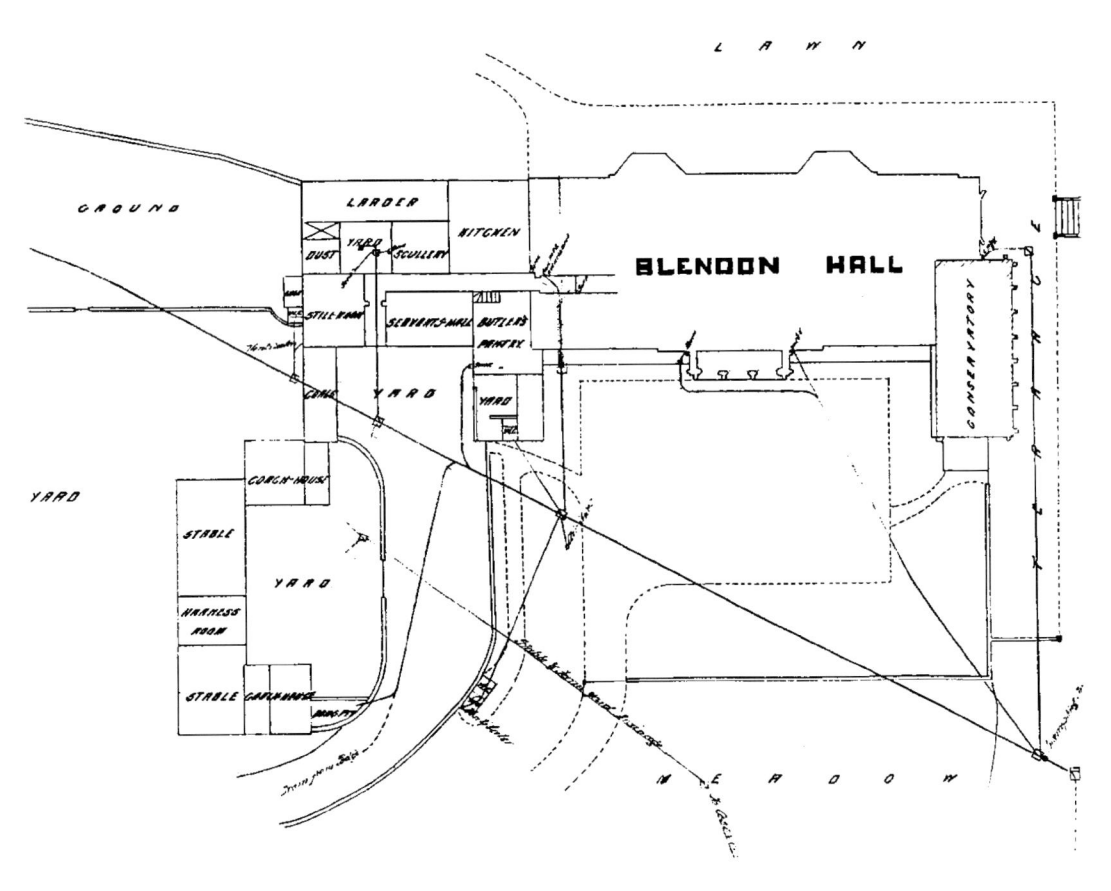

Fig 57. Drainage Map 1898 Details of the domestic part of the hall are clearly shown.
(Bexley Local Studies)

The Americans are coming!

The first document to come down to us from Anna Jay's period at the Hall is a drainage map.[191] It was originally commissioned by her husband but is dated 31st August 1898. The plan shows intended drains and flows of water. However it also details the rooms in the domestic (north) end of the Hall and it appears that the plans are mainly connected with sorting out the drainage in that part of the Hall. As a result of the map we gain a good insight into the alterations that Smith undertook and the general layout of this part of the Hall. Whilst the main farm buildings are excluded from the map we can see the dairy and arbour, kitchen, laundry and drying ground. The stable yard is also detailed – showing coach houses, stables and harness room. Then in the north end of the Hall proper we have the larder, scullery, kitchen, stillroom and butler's pantry (with stairs marked going down to the cellars) and an inner yard. The conservatory (at the south of the Hall) with its seven bays is also clearly drawn. Frustratingly we have no details showing the main rooms. However, outside in the grounds we have the terrace, pathway lawn and meadow shown as well as references on the drain lines such as 'to cesspool in meadow' (this cesspit still exists in a back garden in The Drive) and 'discharges into lake' and 'drain from lodge'.

So what are we to make of this document? It certainly demonstrates some of the issues faced by the large house owner and the associated costs of removing waste from such an extensive area. Jay at the least had a lake he could discharge into – but it required some very long drainage runs to get to it! It provides our only clear 'map' of the domestic end of the Hall (complemented by the aerial photo of the Hall) and confirms the artefacts that have been retrieved from some of the back gardens in Beechway.

We can now turn to Anna Jay's children and their respective families. Her son, William was a barrister-at-law as well as becoming a major and receiving an OBE. He had had connections with Germany (his father was German) - but clearly this was not an issue when war broke out. In 1925, his daughter, Mrs Keown, who was resident in Australia, had her daughter Jane baptised at Saint Mary's in Bexley as she had given birth whilst visiting the U.K.[192] We have a photograph of Mrs Jay, William's wife and her daughter Mrs Keown and her other daughter, Anne.[193] Major William was resident at White Lodge, Datchet, Buckinghamshire at the time of his mother's death.

Anna Jay's eldest daughter Anna was married to Brigadier-General Edmund John Phipps Hornby VC, CB, CMG. Phipps Hornby (1857 – 1947) was described at one time as being the 'best-looking' general in the British army. He saw service in the Royal Horse Artillery in the South African War (1898 – 1902) and was mentioned in dispatches. He then won the Victoria Cross at Sanna's Post on March 31st 1900 for rescuing the guns of 'Q' Battery under fire from the Boers

The Americans are coming!

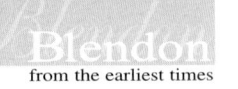

lined up on a ridge overlooking a river and the following order was issued:

> The Field Marshal Commanding-in-Chief, after careful consideration of the report upon the gallant and daring conduct of "Q" Battery, R.H.A., at the action of Sanna's Post, deems that where all 'were equally brave and distinguished', no special selection can be made for the grant of the Victoria Cross. Lord Roberts has therefore been pleased to direct that one officer shall be selected by the officers, one N. C. officer by the N.C. officers, and two gunners or drivers by the gunners and drivers, for the decoration under Article 19, Royal Warrant".

"The following are the selections:-

Major Edmund John Phipps-Hornby

No. 47511 Serjeant Charles Parker

No. 70062 Gunner Isaac Lodge

No. 33286 Driver Henry Glascock".[194]

On his return to Bexley, the celebrations and welcome given to him were one of the notable events of Anna Jay's life, as she would recall in her old age.[195] His Victoria Cross is kept at the Royal Regiment of Artillery Museum "Firepower" at Woolwich.[196] The Phipps Hornbys lived at Hazelwood House on Shooters Hill – a substantial property opposite Shrewsbury Lane, which was later demolished.

In 1914, at the outbreak of war, Edmund Phipps Hornby went to France with the "Old Contemptibles". This was the original British Expeditionary Force that saw service in the early months of the war notably in the Mons and Le Cateau area and for which they were all decorated with the coveted Mons Star decoration.

Fig 58. Brigadier General Edmund Phipps-Hornby
(Courtesy of the Royal Artillery Institution)

The Americans are coming!

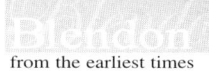

There are two stories on the Blendon/ Hazelwood connection. The first concerns a chow dog. Mrs Jay kept, and exhibited, chow dogs (see Figure 3, 64, 65 and 68). In the mid 1920s two of these animals were especially remembered:

> "Koko was a brown male chow – a friendly animal and the female was a pale cream animal – somewhat reserved but quite affectionate once used to one."

There is a photo extant of the Hall from the south side of the top lake and the figures on the further side of the lake possibly include Mrs Jay, two children, two servants and, sitting in the shade of an oak tree one or two of these animals. Mrs Jay gave a chow dog to her daughter at Shooters Hill. Shortly after moving there, the dog disappeared. The phone then rang and it was Blendon Hall, saying that the dog had turned up there – it had walked all the way 'back home'. Interestingly, a set of candlestick telephones were retrieved from the bottom of a garden in The Drive (still having remnants of the Hessian sack on them) about two feet below ground and we are told that these are likely to have been used in a property of the size and grandeur of the Hall or one of its associated buildings.[197] Why someone should have deposited them in the lake (as it then was) is a mystery. Were they stolen or dumped in haste for more convenient recovery at a later time?

Fig 59. Candlestick Telephones – found buried on the estate.

The Americans are coming!

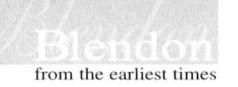

The other story of the Blendon Hall/ Hazelwood link is a postcard sent from the Hall in August 1912 to Miss Smith at Hazelwood. Rose Smith (see Chapter 10) worked in the laundry at Hazelwood and at the time Hazelwood did the laundry for Blendon. The message tells the tale:

> Dear Miss Smith
>
> I do not know whether you unpack the linen hamper or not, but I should be so much obliged to see whether I have sent a pair of stockings in mistake. They will have a red J on top of hem. If you can please return them in today's hamper or post them and I will return you postage.
>
> Yours truly
>
> F M Lainsheer

The Phipps-Hornbys moved to Sonning in Berkshire late on – declining, as did all the children – to take on the Hall.

Mrs Jay's second daughter, Sophie Emily (1871-1938) married on September 10th 1910 at St Mary's Church, Bexley Reginald Mandeville Rodwell (1862 - 1937), a Colonel in the Royal Artillery. (See Appendix III) The Hall had already had connections with the Royal Artillery (Desaguliers and Pattison in the eighteenth and early nineteenth century). We are told that the Royal Artillery band would play for parties at Hazelwood.

Mrs Jay's third daughter, Emma Marie Louise Jay (1876-1950) (known always as 'Miss Jay') never married. She was described as a no-nonsense, practical woman, dressed in brogues and tweed shirt (she may be the woman depicted in Figure 3 in the Preface). She dabbled in chickens and played golf. During the privations of the First World War, she was prepared to skin rabbits on the estate. She was awarded the VAD and the Royal Red Cross second-class decoration for her services in the war. She was also Chairman of the Bexley women's branch of the Conservative & Unionist Association.[198] It was Miss Jay who wrote the reference for Alfred Shrimpton (the odd job man at Blendon) only a few weeks after the death of her mother in 1929. (See Chapter 10) It would seem that Miss Jay moved to Berkshire after her mother's death, along with the lady's maid, Janet Munro – and her chow dogs. However, she is buried with her mother, father and sister, Sophie, in the Jay tomb at St. Mary's, Bexley.

From the memories and recollections of contemporaries and their descendants, we can now build a picture of life at the Hall at the turn of the twentieth century.

The Americans are coming!

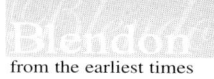

We know that Mrs Jay liked to entertain – and that this would put demands on the staff at the Hall. She certainly would ensure a lavish spread for guests and the following is a typical breakfast for gentlemen guests:

> "In addition to cereals, toast, marmalade, there would be ham, hard-boiled eggs and fish (usually smoked haddock or kipper fillets) or devilled chicken drumsticks." In latter years, Mrs Jay breakfasted in her room and always had hominy – a cereal beloved of Americans – similar to porridge, but quite thin.

We also know that Mrs Jay had a very sweet tooth and loved to eat honey pancakes, and mince pies without the pastry base! We have some dinner plates from the Hall (see illustration) – very colourful and bright!

Mrs Jay also always invited the West Kent Battalion of the Boys Brigade to hold its annual display on August Bank Holidays at Blendon. At this event, the various companies competed for the honour of holding the colours. Until 1927 – for over 25 years – Mrs Jay would present the trophies to the boys and at the presentation ceremony she would ask them to return the following year. Boy Scouts and other young people's organisations were always invited to camp or hold gatherings at Blendon.[199]

Fig 60. The Blendon Game Larder. This little building stood across the road from where Bridgen School was located on the north boundary of the Estate. (Bexley Local Studies)

The Americans are coming!

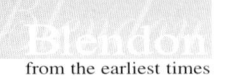

Another big day at the Hall was July 4th – American Independence Day. This is best described in the words of Miss Hazel Hall, daughter of Malsie Walker, who worked as an assistant cook for Mrs Jay towards the end of Mrs Jay's life:

> "To celebrate American Independence Day (4th July) she (Mrs Jay) would hold a huge outdoor party for the locals with a children's party in the afternoon. My mother and brother had attended this as children then my mother had worked to provide the food for this as an adult. There were lots of sandwiches, cakes etc. and games and competitions and races for the children before the adults joined in the evening and a good time was had by all."

We think on these occasions the American national anthem would be played and the Stars and Stripes would fly on the flagpole. This flagpole has survived to this day in the back garden of a property in Cedar Grove – not far where it originally stood on the northern borders of the estate where Blendon parade now stands. There were also close ties with Bridgen School on the northeast border of the Estate. There is an extant photograph of school children and two teachers from Bridgen on a day out in the 1920's at Blendon. One of the teachers is referred to as "Mrs Jay". May Johnson (the aunt of Bob Johnson in Chapter 10) attended the school in the 1910s and her school prizes have been preserved.

In 1909 the Finance Act (Lloyd George's Finance Act) meant that a survey of households throughout the country was undertaken to establish the value of properties. The inspectors visited Blendon in 1912 and we were hoping that they had produced sketch maps of the Hall building itself to give us an accurate

Fig 61. The Hall from the east. Vanes and cupolas are visible as detailed in Chapter 7
(Bexley Local Studies)

Fig 62. The Avenue looking south over the little bridge between the lakes.

Fig 63. The Inner Library at Blendon showing the sham books.

Fig 64. Betty and Irene Phipps Hornby on the steps at Blendon.

Fig 65. Irene Phipps Hornby in the snow at Blendon.

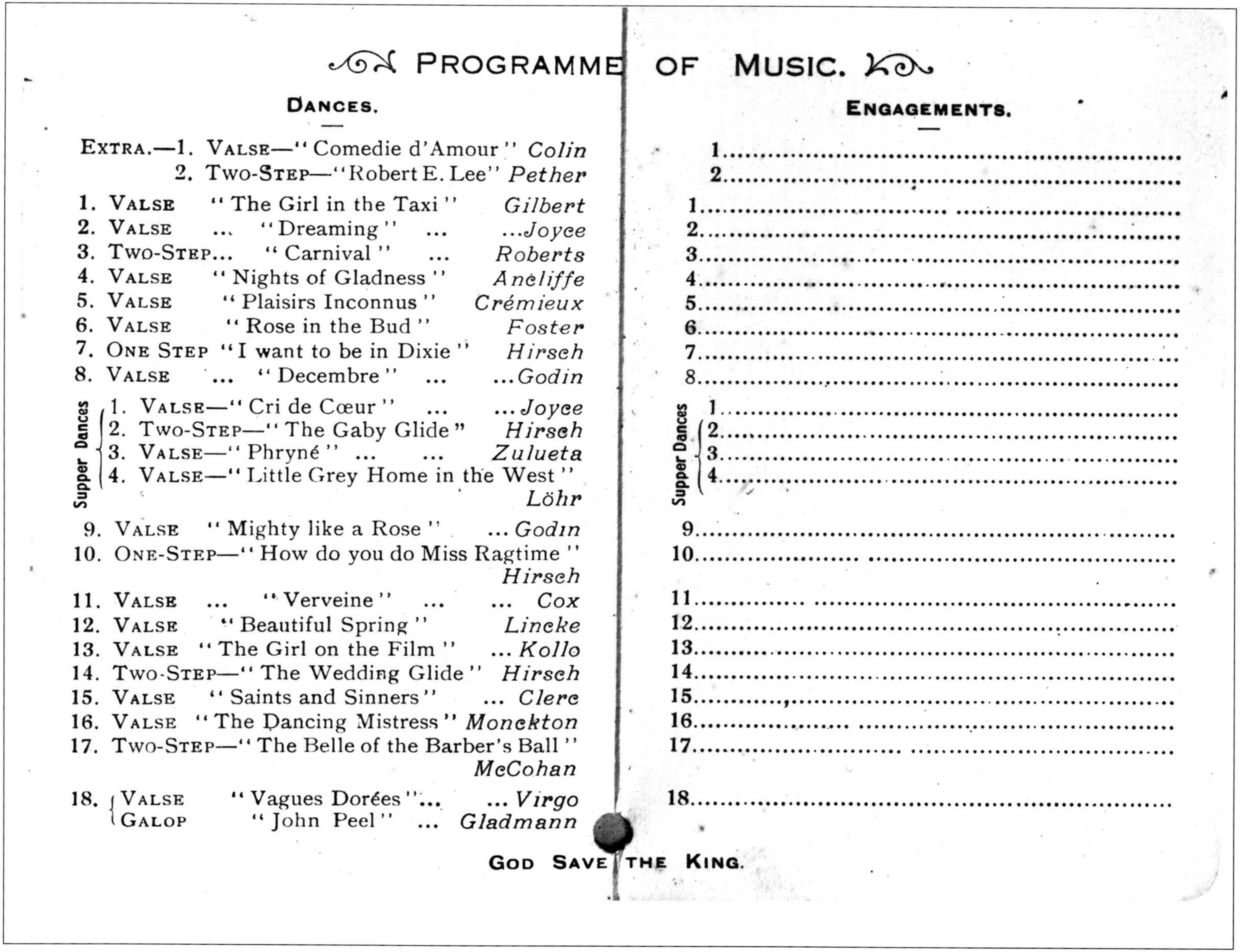

PROGRAMME OF MUSIC.

DANCES.

EXTRA.—1. VALSE—"Comedie d'Amour" *Colin*
    2. TWO-STEP—"Robert E. Lee" *Pether*

1. VALSE "The Girl in the Taxi"   *Gilbert*
2. VALSE ... "Dreaming" ... *Joyce*
3. TWO-STEP... "Carnival"   ... *Roberts*
4. VALSE "Nights of Gladness"   *Ancliffe*
5. VALSE "Plaisirs Inconnus"   *Crémieux*
6. VALSE "Rose in the Bud"   *Foster*
7. ONE STEP "I want to be in Dixie"   *Hirsch*
8. VALSE ... "Decembre"   ... *Godin*

Supper Dances
{
1. VALSE—"Cri de Cœur" ... *Joyce*
2. TWO-STEP—"The Gaby Glide"   *Hirsch*
3. VALSE—"Phryné" ...   *Zulueta*
4. VALSE—"Little Grey Home in the West"   *Löhr*
}

9. VALSE "Mighty like a Rose"   ...*Godin*
10. ONE-STEP—"How do you do Miss Ragtime"   *Hirsch*
11. VALSE ... "Verveine" ... ... *Cox*
12. VALSE "Beautiful Spring" ... *Lineke*
13. VALSE "The Girl on the Film" ...*Kollo*
14. TWO-STEP—"The Wedding Glide"   *Hirsch*
15. VALSE "Saints and Sinners"   ... *Clere*
16. VALSE "The Dancing Mistress"   *Monckton*
17. TWO-STEP—"The Belle of the Barber's Ball"   *McCohan*
18. { VALSE "Vagues Dorées" ... *Virgo*
  GALOP "John Peel" ... *Gladmann*

GOD SAVE THE KING.

ENGAGEMENTS.

1. ....
2. ....

1. ....
2. ....
3. ....
4. ....
5. ....
6. ....
7. ....
8. ....

Supper Dances
{
1. ....
2. ....
3. ....
4. ....
}

9. ....
10. ....
11. ....
12. ....
13. ....
14. ....
15. ....
16. ....
17. ....
18. ....

Fig 66. Dance card from Blendon in 1913.

Fig 67. Rover, Morris Cowley, Rover and Buick outside Blendon – c1923

Fig 68. Collection of Chow dogs with Irene and husband H.F. Lucas – 1927

The Americans are coming!

picture of the interior layout. It was not to be. However, their description is helpful (compare with 1833 inventory, 1863 and 1929 descriptions) and it reads as follows.[200]

> "Blendon Hall" Mansion and Grounds – 85 acres 9 roods 22 perches. Description: Well built Brick Built & Slate and Stucco Mansion – well planned and in 1st rate order – Tudor Style of Architecture – about 200 years old – Stabling in fair order – Farm building do – 85? acres of undulating parkland well timbered – Many trees mainly Spanish Chestnut of fine growth – Wall kitchen gardens in splendid condition – No Gas or Electric Light – Cesspool Drainage – Main Water – All in good order. Desirable property - Timber mostly old of little commercial value.
>
> Gross value: £19,000
>
> Description: **Ground floor accommodation** Entrance Hall (large square)
>
> **Right:** Inner hall. Staircase and wc. (Front): Full sized billiard room. Music room (side). Library. Drawing room (middle)
>
> **Left:** Back: Dining room, Front: Morning room, Back: Housekeeper's room, Front: Butler's bedroom, Front: Butler's pantry
>
> Servants' hall, kitchen, scullery range of larders. Servants' kitchen and bathroom. Back? 2 coalhouses. Four servants' bedrooms reached by secondary staircase.
>
> **First Floor:** Landing small. **Right:** front bedroom and dressing room. Lavatory. Boudoir. Large bedroom (communicates). **Left:** four bedrooms? Bathroom Twelve bedrooms? bath in one boudoir – wc   **Top floor:** Seven bedrooms. Night nursery? **In roof:** Two bedrooms and stove.
>
> **Stabling:** Two coach houses, seven stalls and horsebox. Harness room. Two bedrooms over. Trap house.
>
> **Farm buildings:** Brick Built & Slate barn and cowsheds Two B&S cowshed. Dung yard with range of pigsties and cowshed round Brick Built & Slate farm stabling. Brick Built & Slate Laundry. Brick Built & Thatch and roughcast dairy. Also glasshouses and walled gardens, lake etc.[201]

After the war one of the horses that towed the cortege of the Unknown Warrior to Westminster Abbey was given to the Estate. This horse was reputedly originally found in the wastes of Ypres and brought over to England to perform its sad task. It was positioned on the nearside of the group of

Fig 69. Warrior the Horse. The painting cost Bowyer just 10 guineas.

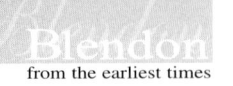

The Americans are coming!

horses. The decision to give the horse to Blendon was in large part based on the Estate's reputation for its care and love of horses. (See Chapter 11)

In 1925, there was the big family gathering as described earlier in the chapter.

But by then Mrs Jay was in her mid-eighties and her health was deteriorating, so that in her twilight years she had to be carried up and down stairs by the chauffeur and butler. Her elder sister, Sophia, also died in that year. As Mrs Jay became more infirm she seldom left the house and when Miss Jay and Mrs Jay's maid went to a show in London, she was heard to lament "Oh cookie, they've all gone and left me alone – quite alone." in spite of there being a staff of twenty!

Fig 70. Family gathering – 1925. Mrs Jay, William's wife, Ethel, and her two daughters Valerie and Robin and Valerie's daughter, Anne. (Courtesy of Kentish Times)

These had also been times of financial worries and, following some concern about investments, she is said to have told the cook that she may have to reduce her wages. The response from the cook was along the lines that she (Mrs Jay) would have to do her own cooking if that were the case! Halls the size of Blendon would have had very high maintenance costs.

At the end, Mrs Jay, bed-ridden and crippled with arthritis, eventually died on February 28th 1929. On Monday March 4th, she was buried at St. Mary's churchyard, Bexley with her husband and close to her parents. Her four children and their families, friends and staff from the Hall attended the funeral. The event was extensively covered in the local paper with the following interesting extract:

> "Mrs. Jay was well loved, not only those connected with her by family ties, but also by those among whom during her long life she found many of her interests. As an indication of the regard in which she was held it may be told that one of the messages

The Americans are coming!

of condolence received by the family was from one in Brighton to whom, in the days when they lived at Queen's Gate-gardens, Mrs. Jay had shewn some kindness. This was a crossing-sweeper lad, known to the family as "Tommy-left-by-the-tide" who used to be specially attentive where the Jays were concerned 26 years ago. They had forgotten about him, but he had not forgotten, and he sent his deepest sympathy."[202]

The photographs of the cortege give us some idea of the size and pomp of the event – the long line of vehicles lining the road and the very sad, grey day it must have been. The newspaper also detailed Anna Jay's will as below:

"Mrs Anna Riggs Jay, of Blendon Hall, Bexley, who died on 28th February last, aged 88 years, widow of C. A. Jay, and daughter of the late William Cunliffe Pickersgill, left unsettled estate of the gross value of £10,812 8s 9d, with net personalty £9,234 16s 7d. Probate of the will, dated 24th December, 1929, with two codicils, has been granted to her son, Major William Cunliffe Pickersgill Jay, of White Lodge, Datchet, Bucks, Brigadier-General Edmund John Phipps Hornby, V.C., G.B., C.M.G., and Basil Henry Wilkinson, of 108a, Cannon Street, E.C., solicitor. The testatrix left £100 each to her grandchildren, Norah Jay, Betty Angela Phipps Hornby, and John Raymond Rodwell, £50 to her great grand-daughter, Anne McKeown, £25 to her god-child, Christa Jay, £25 to her secretary, Miss Winifred Madelaine Atkins, if in her service at her death, £50 to her butler, George Fryers, £100 to her maid, Janet Monro, if in her service at her death, £20 to Mrs. Woods, £10 to her bailiff, Peter McGradie (sic), £10 each to her servants, Henry Johnson, Alfred Medhurst, Samuel Prior, and Samuel Walker, £50 to the Cottage Hospital Bexley, £100 each to the executors of the will, £500 each to her children, £150 each to her two sons-in-law and her daughter-in-law, and the residue of the property to her children in equal shares."[203]

So ended the Pickersgill/Jay link with Blendon – which extended over sixty-five years.

And really, this is the end of the Hall and Estate as it had been for centuries. With Anna Jay's death, the staff either retired or moved on – and the whole infrastructure of mutual dependency was gone. But before we move on, it is appropriate to understand some more about the staff that worked at the Hall over the years.

Mrs Jay's Funeral Cortege in March 1929

Fig 71. The cortege outside the Hall.

Fig 72. The cortege arriving at Bexley with St Mary's Church on the right...

Fig 73. The cortege passing out of the Estate at the top of Beechway.

Fig 74. The cortege lined up on Blendon Road.

Chapter Ten

The Staff at Blendon

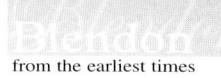

In July 2000, when we held our first public talk on Blendon, we showed a photograph of the staff at Blendon in about 1900. We knew none of their names. The next photograph that we displayed showed a cow in the foreground, the Lake with the Hall in the background. This picture was originally included in the D.C.Bowyer Sales Catalogue of the Estate. Jim Bowyer had been able to identify the cow – a light roan, name it – 'Crowhurst' – and give its value at the time of the farming stock sale in September 1929 – £22 10 shillings. We could name a cow but not any of the people in the picture. The irony was not lost on the audience.

Therefore as part of the follow-up to the event, we were determined to give these people names – and if possible a place in the written story of Blendon. We asked the late Roger Wright, at the News Shopper newspaper to write a review on the research to date.[204] At the end of the article we appealed for anyone who had a relative who lived or worked on the Estate to contact us. The article appeared in thirty-four area editions of the paper – and we waited for the phone to ring!

There had been a few references to other staff at Blendon down the years. Perhaps most notably in May 1738, when Charles Wesley led the conversion of the Delamottes, including their minister – the Reverend Henry Piers of Bexley – two maidservants and their gardener. There are no names – just positions. Other names appear later in the records as 'living at the Hall' in the censuses, but only those in the late nineteenth/early twentieth century appeared to give any scope for an insight into individual's lives.

And then the phone rang. As with all responses to an appeal of this nature some calls proved more useful than others. What was interesting was that two callers, on consecutive nights, mentioned the same surname: Beckenham. Another name raised was Smith – and it appeared the two families were related in some way. After discussion with the two contacts over a period of months, it was possible to create a united family tree that showed them sharing the same great-grandparents named Smith in the early nineteenth century. We were also able to put the contacts in touch with each other – which was a great bonus. They also

The Staff at Blendon

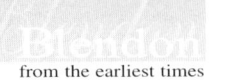

Fig 75. Staff at Blendon – 1900. Why they look so miserable is not clear. Some have suggested it was the way people set their faces for photographs at this time, others have said that they had to stay stock still during the long exposure. Another suggestion is that they were not being paid 'overtime' for this sitting! (Bexley Local Studies)

identified, separately, two people in the photo. One is the boy in the front row, third from the right. He is Albert Smith, who emigrated to Australia in 1921.

The other person identified is his aunt, Ellen Beckenham (née Smith) who is fifth from the left in the middle row. She was married to Alfred Beckenham, who was the Head Gardener at Blendon and lived at East Lodge. (This was confirmed by the Finance Act survey in 1912). In the 1881 Census we have the following entry: Alfred Beckenham (gardener) – 30, Ellen Beckenham (his wife) 29 and their three children: Helen Maria (5 years), Elsie (2 years) and Alice Maude (7months) at the Lodge, Blendon. All were born at Bexley. Two of Alfred Beckenham's brothers are also mentioned – Edward (an unemployed plasterer) and Walter (a florist).[205]

The other individual, who merited a special mention, although not in the group photo, was Sophie Beckenham. Sophie was the nursemaid to the Jays in the early part of the twentieth century and then after the sale of the estate she lived

The Staff at Blendon

in Beechway with her sister (Nellie). She was given a beautiful ornament on her departure from the Jay household (see photo). Rose Smith (Albert's sister) was a parlourmaid at Hazelwood for the Phipps Hornby's and was the recipient of the postcard in Chapter 9. Her mother worked in the laundry at Blendon.

One suspects there are other Smiths and Beckenhams in the photo – but definite identification is not yet possible. Perhaps further study of the 1901 census will tell us more.

Among the other information received following the July 2000 talk was a reference to 'Bexley Mosaic' Workers Educational Association 1977. The existence of the extract

Fig 76. The Beckenhams at West Lodge – 1890s

was kindly provided by one of the audience, and in Chapter 2 of the booklet there is an account of service at Blendon Hall. There are some factual inaccuracies in the text, but the account of service at the Hall is fascinating.[206]

In Service at Blendon Hall

"A friend of mine, who was born in 1885, spent three months in the year of 1907 as a kitchen maid at Blendon Hall. It was then in the possession of Mrs. Carl Jay, an American lady, who lived there with her two daughters, her son being in Germany. From the two postcards I was allowed to see it seems to have been an ugly building. The front elevation was very flat with a large central porch and four sash windows, on the second floor, three small windows over the centre and the rest of the windows were hidden by crenellations. Above this were attics, but their windows were completely hidden by further crenellations. My friend, who slept in the attic, remarked that they could see nothing but roof from their windows. The whole front was covered by ampelopsis, a type of creeper that turned a lovely colour in the autumn. The rear elevation also had many windows and two large built-out bays,

The Staff at Blendon

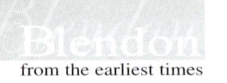

Fig 77. Vase. A gift from the Hall to Sophie Beckenham

from ground to roof. This part of the house overlooked one of the lakes, which must have disappeared when the estate was built over about 1936.

From the postcards it would seem that the house stood where Cedar Grove is today. At the top of Beechway is a stretch of very old wall, belonging to the garden of No.1. It is believed that this is where the kitchen garden was. In Blendon Road are two very old houses, Nos. 1 and 2 Jays Cottages. This was where one of the gardeners lived. Opposite are two houses, now modernised, where the coachmen lived.

The staff of Blendon Hall during my friend's stay were:- The butler, two footmen, house-boy and odd man, the housekeeper, three housemaids, the cook, kitchen maid, scullery maid, ladies' maid, several gardeners, the coachman and several men connected with the stables. My friend never did know how many outside staff were employed.

The Staff at Blendon

A typical day in the life of a kitchen maid could begin at 6 a.m. when she and the scullery maid, who shared an attic bedroom, got up and went down the back stairs to the kitchen.

The kitchen fire would have been already lit by the odd man, but the kitchen maid had to keep it stoked. She would scrub the tables and floors and then get the servants breakfast and take a cup of tea to the cook. She would then help cook prepare the dining-room for breakfast. She then prepared and cooked most of the servants hall dinner at twelve midday, the scullery maid doing all the vegetables and washing up, of course; The butler and housekeeper took meat in the servants hall; the butler doing the carving but they then went to the housekeeper's room for the 'sweet and cheese' – the houseboy would serve this (and also their breakfast which they would take in the housekeeper's room).

The dining room lunch would be served at 1 p.m.; the kitchen maid would help with the cooking and dishing up. Then the tables and floors would all be scrubbed again and also the huge larders, then everything covered in muslin. Mrs. Jay used to come down to inspect everything now and then. Afterwards, the kitchen staff would go upstairs to wash and put on clean print dresses and have an hour to themselves until it was time to prepare tea in (a) the dining room, (b) the housekeepers room (c) the servants hall and (d) the kitchen. Then it would be time to prepare the dining room dinner for 8 p.m. and afterwards the servants' supper. After cleaning up in the kitchen, it would be time for bed.

Mrs. Jay and her two daughters used to do a lot of entertaining and Saturdays and Sundays were especially busy. My friend remembers the kitchen floor being covered with dirty dishes at 11 p.m. and having to give a helping hand to the scullery maid. She also remembers the under-housemaid scrubbing the back stairs at 6 p.m.

My friend was allowed to have every other Sunday afternoon and evening off – after lunch until 10 p.m. She remembers walking over the fields to Blackfen and getting a tram at Wellington Avenue to London to a music hall with the footman!

She also remembers the horse-buses that used to run up Danson Road from the Crook Log to the Mansion Gates. She remembers that the lane down to St. John's Church at Bexley was very narrow.

My friend said that she never did go into any rooms at the front of the house. She only knew the kitchen, back stairs and attics ... however, while she was there, the butler, who had been in Mrs. Jay's employ for many years, died, and was laid out in state in the front hall with lighted candles at the four corners. The staff were allowed to pay their respects. The head footman was then made butler.

My friend then left after three months of purgatory!"

The butler in the text is probably George Harper, whose granddaughter had also contacted us (see photo). He had lived in West Lodge and had been given a clock as a wedding gift and a prayer book belonging to William Pickersgill.

The Staff at Blendon

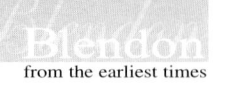

Sadly, he died very young, at the age of 45 of cancer and was clearly much loved by the Jays.

Another character to 'emerge' from this time was Peter McGready. Peter has been described, by those who were young lads at the time, as a 'tall fearsome Scot with whiskers, wearing gaiters, jodhpurs and a flat cap with a shotgun over his arm'. McGready was the last bailiff of the estate and lived in the cottage, which still stands between Bladindon Drive and The Drive. Jim Bowyer, as a young boy, would look in through the kitchen window of this cottage and chat to Mrs McGready as she polished the silverware or baked a cake. He particularly remembers her rosy cheeks and the frilly cap she wore on her head. McGready would always address Jim as 'Master Douglas' and it was McGready who was the contact for the sale of agricultural machinery in the autumn of 1929 (see Chapter 11). Afterwards he was given a role as keeper of Bexley Woods. Apparently he could also spit 'bacca' across a bar into a spittoon – a skill not often demonstrated in pubs today!

Fig 78. George Harper – 1890s. A loyal servant to the Pickersgills and Jays for a number of years.

By the end of 2000, we thought we had at least begun the process of understanding about those who worked at the Hall. We knew by then about an array of people who worked as nursemaids, laundry assistants, gardeners and a cowman and also a little about the butler and bailiff.

Then in April 2001, the following document was passed to us by Miss Hazel Hall who had come to our talk at Hall Place:

> "My mother went to work at Blendon Hall in 1926 at the age of 17 to improve her career as a cook. She had already worked for 3 years at the "Mount Mascal" estate in North Cray. The salary was £40.00 per year plus board and lodging. I believe the food was adequate but the accommodation was primitive – sharing an attic bedroom with one, sometimes two, other maids – the room was on the second floor, unheated

The Staff at Blendon

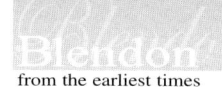

and without lighting so candles proved a fire risk.

On one occasion the maids, fearful of being caught in an inferno practised getting out of the very small window into a flat roof below – my mother was very small about 7 stone in weight and got out and back in – without difficulty – the other lass was built on more generous lines but was very determined to try – and became well and truly stuck and it needed several of the men servants to bend the frame and thus release her - she returned to her native Suffolk soon after!!

There were three bathrooms at the Hall but none were permitted to use them so these girls had to haul buckets of boiling water up to a tin bath in the bedroom."

The servants wore a uniform. My mother's was a mauve check dress with white apron and cap. I believe the housemaids wore black dresses and small white aprons; kitchen staff wore large bib aprons. I understand there were a staff of twenty servants – 10 "inside" and 10 "outside" (but these were fed with the inside staff in the staff dining Hall).

"In the kitchen there was the cook (in my mother's time a formidable lady) of Dutch descent – a Miss Guilder (Barbara) who was very good at sewing and made her own coat, an assistant cook, (my mother – Malsie Walker), kitchen maid and scullery maid. There was a chauffeur – Mr. Hawes (who lived in the lodge on the corner of the drive) – a gardener – Mr. McGready (pronounced MacCready) who lived in a house in a driveway off Bladindon Drive, The butler Mr Fryers who lived with his wife and two sons and a little daughter in a house close by the "Blackbirds" public house – and next door to him lived Mrs. Winnie Lynch – the laundress (a boiler no washing machines in those days) who used a huge copper and a three legged "Dolly" to pound the clothes and a washboard (of skiffle fame) to remove any stains. Her adult daughter was her assistant. Opposite in "Jays Cotts" lived one of the assistant gardeners – a Mr. Walker (no relation) and his family. A further stockman was a Mr. Medhurst who lived in Vale Place cottages in Bridgen Road – he cared for the pigs and was also a gardener (in later life he lived a few doors from me – was blind but still able to draw a straight furrow). Although my mother's home was nearby in the village of Bridgen she had to "live in" as the maids had to be downstairs and ready to start work at 6 a.m. The first task was to rake out and re lay the fires – the cooking was all done by fire – there was no gas or electricity thus no cooker. There was also an odd-job man – Alfred Shrimpton – whose job it was to take out the cinders and bring in the sticks and coal."

Some of this extract corroborates the information from the Bexley Mosaic extract. This is the very end of the Jay era and elsewhere in the article we hear tell of Mrs Jay's fading health.

Then in May 2001 Mr Bob Johnson contacted Local Studies to offer some books from Bridgen School, which were given as prizes to his aunt, May Johnson. There was already a photograph of Mr Johnson's father and grandfather donated in 1993 and his grandfather also appeared in the composite photo – back row, 4th from right. We visited Mr and Mrs Johnson and he

The Staff at Blendon

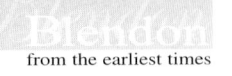

kindly provided the following:

"My grandfather, Henry James Johnson, moved to Blendon from his home at Lamarsh in Essex around 1873 and started work at Blendon Hall as a gardener. He stayed until his death on 17th April 1925. The family occupied Vine Cottage which was next to The Three Blackbirds pub and which was demolished, I believe in the 1960's to make way for the pub car park. May Johnson, his youngest daughter, (my aunt), continued to work at Blendon Hall and probably went to live in until she married Alfred Shrimpton on 15th May 1929.

My father Alfred James Johnson, started work as a garden boy at the Hall in 1905 aged 14. The photo shows Henry James and Alfred James with donkey, mowing the grass at the Hall.

Fig 79. Extract of Testimony to Alfred Shrimpton written by Miss Jay. This extract provides a fascinating 'job description' on a large estate as this time.

Fig 80. Henry James Johnson and Alfred James Johnson with donkey, mowing the grass at the Hall c1910
(Bexley Local Studies)

The Staff at Blendon

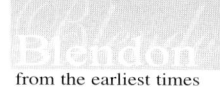

My father mentioned that when he was duty gardener, which entailed stoking the greenhouse boiler late in the evening, he used to take a short cut across the lawns in front of the house instead of following the prescribed longer route out of sight of the house. Continued use of the short cut used to cause wear to the grass so Humphreys, the Head Gardener, stretched a rope between two bushes about a foot above ground with the result that my father fell over and rolled down an adjacent bank. He used the proper route thereafter.

As an indicator of how times have changed I recall my father saying that he used to hear the post horn of the Dover stage coach as he lay in bed at night. (It was the stage wagon as at that time it presumably carried only parcels). I used to think he was pulling my leg until, years later, I found that the GPO had stopped using the railway for mails around 1889 and reverted to the stage because rail charges were too high."

Mr and Mrs Johnson were also able to provide a number of photographs – including the ones of Mrs Jay's cortege and the aerial photo on the front of this book, as well as the testimony to Alfred Shrimpton – the odd job man who had married May Johnson – Bob Johnson's aunt.

One other story that has recently come to light is the tradition at Blendon that when a pig littered, the runt was given to the youngest member of the 'outside' staff. We have been told that one of the last occasions this happened the youngster placed the runt in a sack and had to keep it at his home in Plumstead for three days before a butcher could be found to slaughter it.

Finally, there is the article from Garden Life, which is reproduced in full in the appendix. Humphreys was an important person in the Blendon story whilst not strictly a member of 'staff'.

There are also a few surviving artefacts that seem more appropriate in this chapter than in any other. There is an oil lamp, which has been passed down in one of the families that came from the Hall. We also have three fragments of ribbed glass thought to be from a wooden – framed glass washboard dating from the early twentieth century that was found in the back garden of a house in Beechway (where the domestic part of the hall was located). From a nearby location a fragment of glazed white interior tile with leaf stem and bud transfer pattern with applied paint was found. This possibly depicts the 1870s Arts and Craft movement influence and is likely to have come from a fireplace surround or possibly a washstand back.[207] We have also recently unearthed an early nineteenth century, finely decorated, clay pipe.

In summary, in just over a year a number of the Blendon staff have emerged

The Staff at Blendon

Fig 81. Glazed tile 1870s

into the light so that their story can be written along with others who owned or tenanted the Hall and were at the other end of the social spectrum. We can only hope that other people will be identified in the photograph and relatives come forward so that their lives and place in the Blendon story can be shared and appropriately told.

Fig 82. Plate from the Hall

Chapter Eleven

Decline, Fall and Transformation
"Enter the Guvnor"

Events moved quickly following Mrs Jay's death. 'For Sale' boards were erected on the borders of the estate within a few weeks. Staff began to move on – with the appropriate references – probably aware that the Estate was about to undergo its most profound change in the hundreds of years that it had existed. Whilst none of the immediate Jay family wanted to take on the Hall and Estate, one senses that they all, and particularly Miss Jay, did everything they could to assist those going through a difficult transition. Messrs Knight, Frank and Rutley drew up a detailed description of the Hall and Estate for the forthcoming sale. As mentioned in Chapter 8, the 1929 document shows few substantial changes to the 1863 sale document drawn up on Oswald Smith's death – except that the Hall was sixty-five years older.

Economically, 1929 was very difficult. In America it was the year of the Great Wall Street Crash and the start of the Depression. Unemployment was high in the UK – times were hard. However, it was also a time of building and investment. Blendon was one of many old private estates that was to be transformed into a residential housing estate. The Vansittart Estate on Blendon's southern borders had been purchased by Ideal Homesteads and was being developed as a huge housing estate. Large tracts of farmland in Bexleyheath, Barnehurst, Welling and Sidcup were already being built on. The sale of the 'Freehold Residential and Building Estate known as Blendon Hall' was held on 1st July 1929. Knight, Frank and Rutley conducted the sale in conjunction with Messrs. Dann and Lucas at Hanover Square in London, at the direction of the Trustees of the late W.C. Pickersgill.[208] D.C.Bowyer, a local builder from Belvedere, who had prospered from land purchase and development around London, purchased the whole Blendon Estate for £29,000.

Bowyer, originally from London and always affectionately known as the Guvnor, had development plans for the Estate drawn up by Mr Rowlands, a young, local architect. The plan showed his intention to retain the bottom lake and the Hall as important features of the new estate. In his copy of the sales catalogue at the auction and in his own literature, Bowyer highlighted the potential economic use of the Hall itself as a school.

Decline, Fall and Transformation

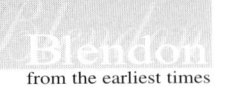

The sale of the contents of the Hall came immediately after the sale of the Estate. Anna Jay's executors ordered the sale. For three days (3rd – 5th July 1929), Knight, Frank and Rutley in conjunction with Messrs. Dann and Lucas, oversaw the sale of items at the Hall from the grand to the very small.[209] A huge diversity of people, from professional buyers to those simply wanting to view what the Hall had contained, must have visited the Hall over those three days. We know that D C Bowyer bought some items. To date, we have been unable to locate a detailed record of the proceedings. However, 'The Record' of July 1929 in its 'News and Notes of the Month' section notes that: 'High prices were given, after spirited bidding for many of the lots offered at the sale of household furniture and effects at Blendon Hall…Remarkable interest was taken in an antique Persian carpet, which started with a small bid and was eventually knocked down for £250.'[210] When it was over, the Hall was a shell with only the larger items to be collected. The intermittent noises of people and removal men taking away their newly purchased belongings too would shortly cease and the Hall would fall silent.

Fig 83. Estate from Danson Road showing sale boards and Boswell's car (Bexley Local Studies)

There would be one more sale – of all the remaining Blendon farming stock, agricultural machinery, equipment and product on 19th September of that year. Catalogues were available from Peter McGreadie at the Gardens, Blendon Hall.[211]

However, this shell of a building provided a wonderful playground for young Jim Bowyer, D.C.Bowyer's eldest son, and his friends.

Jim recalls:

> "We would play in the Hall and run around the place. At night we'd sleep in the old library, (the south end of the Hall), and there'd be all those books on shelves from floor to ceiling. Actually, they were false books – (the sham books of the 1833 inventory).
>
> The old building used to bang a lot – a door or window would crash shut at night.

Decline, Fall and Transformation

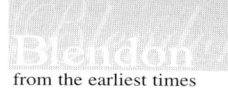

The toilets were fun. They were 'pedestal' toilets and you sat on them and pulled a pedestal to flush. They were all cracked and old - you thought you'd be swept away with all the water pressure!"

Out on the estate, Jim and his friends created a floating raft made of drums and planks, strapped together. On one occasion they frightened off some people on the lake with their horseplay – something recalled years later by a guest on BBC Radio 4's Desert Island Discs! Jim's younger brothers, Charles and Bill, were able to play on the estate. Other youngsters were enjoying the estate as well – Ron Anthony and his younger brother Roy were two of them. Their father was site manager working for their uncle, Arthur Buck on the Blendon Drive plots. Ron and Roy fell in the lower lake and were saved from being sucked into the sluices by their Alsatian dog, Rufus. The lake was always a hazard – even more so in its half drained state when it proved a magnet to young children.

In the winter people would skate on the ice-covered lakes with a ladder to hand for rescuing those who fell in. We also have a comment on a turn of the century postcard stating that Blendon is 'a great place to skate'.

In 1931, Jim Bowyer, started work at the West Lodge, which was used as the Estate office. He stayed there, except for the war years, until 1985. It was also agreed during this time that it would be appropriate to have Warrior the horse painted. We have copies of the correspondence between the artist, W.A. Clark of Hanover Road, Tottenham and D.C. Bowyer in January and February 1931. The result was a painting 24 inches by 20 inches, which is owned by Charles Bowyer. The total cost of the undertaking was ten guineas – which included delivery to Heron Hill works. The artist is directed to the Bailiff for viewing and painting Warrior – and he is also advised to catch a 132 bus from Bexley station to reach the Estate. 70 years on the same number bus still plies its trade to Blendon. It was requested that Warrior be painted with a landscape background. Because of Warrior's special status it was necessary to get permission from the War Office when it was time for him to be put down.

Meanwhile, the Estate was being developed apace. Bowyer had not intended to build all the properties himself but to sell off plots to local builders. He had however set strict standards for the quality of properties to be developed and no property was to be sold for less than £650. 'The Guvnor' produced his sales catalogue in 1929. Jim Bowyer recalls it was his job to pull all the blinds down on the windows for the Hall photograph on the front of the detailed insert in the catalogue – a task that took a long time! The grass was also specially mowed for the photograph.

Decline, Fall and Transformation

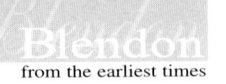

The Estate was developed in a haphazard fashion and there is an interesting aerial photograph of the area from this time, which neatly contrasts the Ideal Homes development to the south with the Blendon Hall Estate.

Fig 84. Aerial photo of development. The Hall is hidden in the trees. Development on The Drive is visible at the top. (Reproduced by kind permission of Simmons Aerofilms).

Bowyer built the quality houses in The Crescent. He also built Cedar Grove. (Pictures of this building activity with the Hall in the background exist.) But other builders did large chunks of the estate: Fred Clarke, Arthur Buck, Bill Neal, George Smith, Pollock and Sheffield all featured. A small red train ran round the estate delivering supplies to where building was active – and recently a small portion of rail has been recovered from a garden in The Drive. Some of the local youngsters played havoc with the railway and pushed carriages into the lake!

Time however, was running out for the Hall itself. Bowyer had advertised widely for a purchaser and for a period of time serious negotiations were underway between himself and two headmasters to create an educational establishment. Sadly, one of the potential purchasers died and the deal fell through and nothing else of substance materialised.

Decline, Fall and Transformation

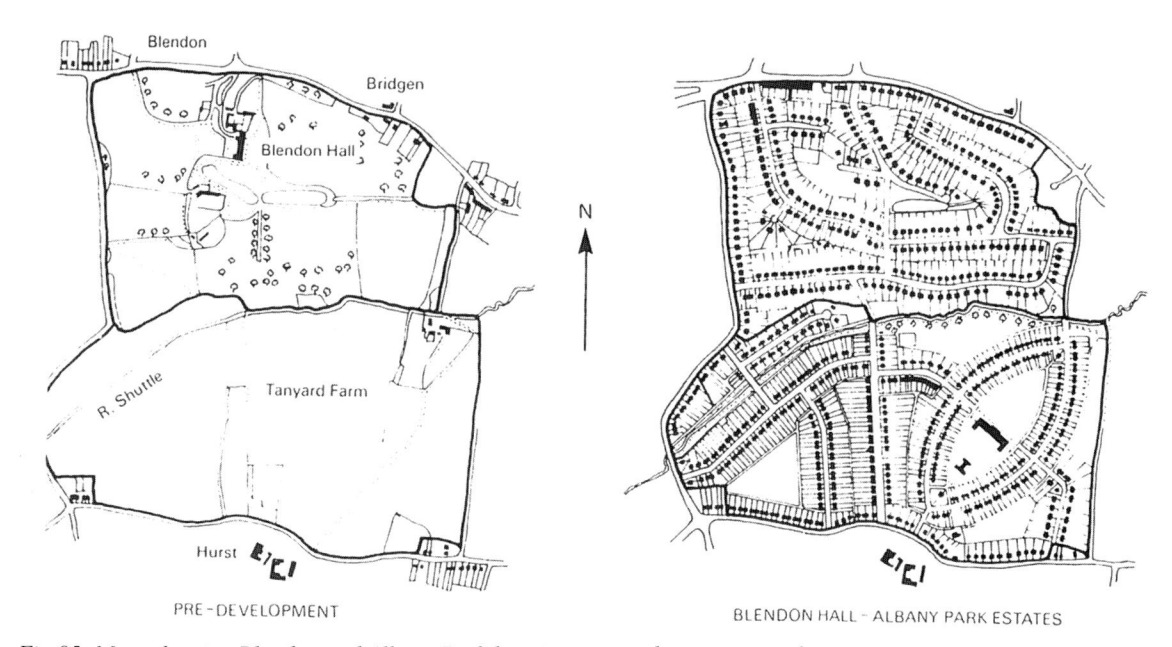

Fig 85. Maps showing Blendon and Albany Park housing estates demonstrating the comparative density of the two estates. Bowyer set a covenant on the minimum selling price of a dwelling built on the estate. (Reproduced by kind permission of Continuum International Publishing Group from 'The Rise of Suburbia' by F.M.L. Thomson, Leicester University Press, 1982 (original drawing by Elaine Butt).

During this time Peter McGready, as bailiff of the estate, showed a group of schoolchildren round the empty hall and one of them particularly remembers the very large kitchen with a huge boiler. The Hall had now been unoccupied for almost five years and it must have suffered from some deterioration during that time. Whilst never vandalised or broken into, the threat of fire was always present and the decision was finally taken to bring it down. This would result in another fifty plus housing plots becoming available in what was to become Beechway and The Sanctuary. It also signalled the end for the top lake – which was drained and became the back gardens of the properties on the south side of The Sanctuary. The services of Rube and Fred Saunders of Woolwich were employed and a number of photographs were taken of the ensuing destruction. These photographs show fixtures and fittings and some of the original architecture. The Hall was levelled and all the material taken out to Plumstead marshes.

But not quite! We have Joan Pollard from Bexleyheath to thank for this recollection:

"I remember my father taking me to Blendon as a young girl in about 1934. There, during the latter stages of the destruction of the Hall Portland stone, marble,

Blendon from the earliest times

Decline, Fall and Transformation

Destruction of Hall in 1934
(Reproduced by kind permission of Topham {Picturepoint})

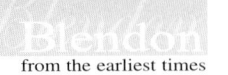

Fig 86.

Fig 87.

Fig 88.

Fig 89.

Decline, Fall and Transformation

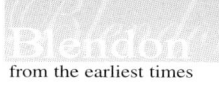

chimney pots were laid out on the lawns. My father bought a chimney pot, which we placed in the middle of our pond in our back garden. It stayed there, until cracked and broken by frost in the 1940s. He also bought a couple of marble slabs, which he cemented into our rock garden."

A number of the fixtures and fittings therefore seem to have survived the Hall's destruction. We have indications that other chimney pots survive (three is the current confirmed tally), four 'toadstools' (which supported a granary store), a flagpole, a sundial, and two gateposts (perhaps those that were mentioned in the Farming Stock sale above). We are sure many other artefacts are still in existence – in gardens off or on the Estate. Sadly, many of the generation who were around at the time of the destruction of the Hall and original building of the Estate, have passed on, so we have often had to rely on hearsay evidence.

By 1936, the estate was on its way to completion. The typical purchase price for a new semi in Beechway was at this time £750 (this was Type "B" on the estate). These were Clarke built houses – 'designed specially for the Up-to-date Housewife'. Some of these properties had some fairly exciting underground cellars to be exploited as shelters in the forthcoming hostilities of World War II.

During the Second World War, enemy action caused damage to properties on the Estate. In the 'Schedule of properties rendered uninhabitable by enemy action for the Borough of Bexley – 19th May 1945' a number of incidents are recorded. Principal damage is listed in Bladindon Drive and in The Drive. The first serious damage occurred in October 1940 at 69 The Drive. It was over two and a half years before the property was repaired. Then in April 1941 number 93 The Drive was totally destroyed and a number of adjacent properties damaged and the occupiers evacuated for repairs as a result of a high explosive bomb. In early 1944 there was some light damage at the west end of Bladindon Drive. Then on the 2nd July 1944, at 6 a.m., a V1 'Flying Bomb' crashed on to the Estate. A large number of properties were so badly damaged as to put them beyond repair in the same part of Bladindon Drive and there were casualties. Damage from this explosion spread as far as The Drive and The Crescent. A number of residents were evacuated in to the Rest Centre at St James Church as a result. Although there was a rule that no dogs were allowed into the Centre, Mr Joe Selby got agreement to bring Sam his dog in and shared a top bunk with him. Sam fidgeted so much that in the middle of the night Mr Selby took him outside to stretch his legs – and have a cigarette himself! A few weeks later, on 6th August 1944 a high explosive bomb caused numbers 42, 44, 48 and 50 Bladindon Drive to be all listed as 'destroyed or so badly damaged that demolition was necessary'. Mrs Carol Linaye recalls this event;

'the bomb landed in an elm tree in Crofton Avenue and the back of our house

Decline, Fall and Transformation

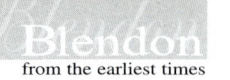

Artefacts from the Estate

Fig 90. Chimney pot reputed to come from the Hall – now an unusual flower pot in a garden on the Estate

Fig 91. 'Toadstool' that supported a granary store

Fig 92. Gatepost. Tradition has it that a haywain struck the post on the way into a field

Fig 93. Part of the track that led to the walled garden

Decline, Fall and Transformation

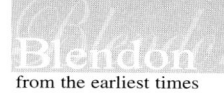

(number 48) was extensively damaged and much of the back of the property was blown down the hill and ended in the River Shuttle. We were safe in our shelter. Our Airedale dog, Sam (the same dog mentioned above) however, had been sitting on the settee when the bomb dropped and was nowhere to be seen. The air raid warden then told us there was some movement under the rubble in the river and our dog emerged, shook himself and was apparently unscathed. All he suffered was the loss of the top of his ear!'

Fig 94. Bomb damage – Bladindon Drive viewed from Crofton Avenue

Mr Ken Batchelder, a local resident in Bexley, recalls as a 15 year old, going out on his bicycle in 1943 searching for shrapnel following a night time raid. He came into Bladindon Drive and found a hole at the junction with Crofton Avenue, which was 'big enough to put a house in' caused by a high explosive bomb. Mercifully on that occasion there seemed relatively little property damage.

In 1944 Iris Brooker visited Chelmer Cottage at the head of The Avenue and the home of Pastor Wood. She recalls,

"Being young I was not too keen on spending Christmas day with them, but I must confess it was a very enjoyable day. There were many trees around. It was very quiet, and the lake very calm. We all sat in the Summerhouse, which was about where they built their second house further down on the left of the lake, and enjoyed the peace, and the lawn going down to the lake. Two swans came up on the lawn and sat there. Later after eating, talking, and seeing Pastor Woods' photos of the building of Chelmer Cottage in all its different stages, we said our good byes and left for home, and what a lovely surprise we had. Everything was covered with deep crisp snow, all the trees white, and everywhere so still and quiet, it must have been nearly midnight, but the snow lit up the night. We walked on to the bridge, the lake was very beautiful, and the very tall trees in the Avenue all white and still. We just stood there silently, drinking in the beauty, and then quietly left and walked home feeling very happy."

Decline, Fall and Transformation

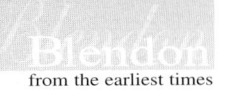

(The summerhouse, a remnant from the Estate has been restored and still exists in a garden on the estate today – although the mechanism that made it revolve so effortlessly no longer supports it)

After the war, Jim Bowyer tells the following story:

> "In 1948, my brother-in-law George Wright came into the office and asked me what I wanted for the lower lake. Well, it wasn't much good to us, so I said, 'A fiver!' So he gave me five pounds – and took it on!"

Whether George Wright came to rue that decision is not clear. But on August 12th 1955 the following article appeared in the Kentish Times:

> **Blendon Lake to be restored?**
>
> **"A plan to restore the lake adjacent to gardens in The Drive and Beechway, Blendon, to its former state, has been outlined by the owner, Mr. G. A. Wright.**
>
> **The history of the lake shows that until approximately 1932 it was part of the Blendon Hall Estate, and the lake then passed into private ownership.**
>
> Today the lake, which is about 150 yds long and 30 yds wide, has become the subject of much discussion and negotiation.
>
> Residents have complained from time to time to both the owner and local authority, that the lake has taken on the appearance of a quagmire and become stagnant.
>
> A further complaint is that unless the lake is restored to something like its former condition the value of their property may well decrease.

Fig 95. Anglers on the Lake at the turn of the century (Bexley Local Studies)

Decline, Fall and Transformation

In addition, residents have been agitating for the lake to be cleaned. Their contention is that in its present state it is injurious to health, although they realise that the title deeds of their property give them no rights over the lake.

Mr G A Wright, in discounting many of the points raised by the residents, said that there was no evidence of injurious effect on the health of those living in the vicinity and that this was supported by the opinion of the Borough Health Department whose representative had visited the site.

Mr Wright also denied that there was any infiltration of injurious substance from the inlet and the Corporation's drains, several of which found contact with the lake.

The crux of the matter was an insufficient inflow of water into the lake area.

He said that a sufficient supply of water had reached the lake until the last few years when with the continued development of the district there had been a general drop in the water level. In consequence the present day water supply in the lake was about only one tenth of the normal inflow of five years ago.

He also made mention of unauthorised dumping of extraneous matter in the lake and said that at one time considerable expense had been incurred by the necessity to unstop the outlet.

Mr Wright then gave an insight into some proposed operations which he hoped would be put in hand in the near future.

Attempts had been made during the last fortnight to dispose of the water remaining in the lake and a trench had been dug at the opposite end below the level of the inlet.

This had resulted in most of the water draining away. What little remained he hoped would be cleared by evaporation in a continued spell of fine weather.

In connection with attempts to clear water from the lake, Mr Wright said it had come to light that a 17 ft. pole pushed into the mud in the centre of the lake had failed to find what he termed an indefinite bottom.

When, however, it became possible to venture on the mud he proposed to treat it with chloride of lime to rid the lake of any offensive element. He also has a plan for the partial filling in of the lake which would eliminate the surrounding area of mud bank and leave a shallow area of water about 2 ft. deep with a clear water course. This would reduce the lake in about two-thirds of its present area.

Further proposals include the permitted tipping of sand and clay which would form a hard core on the bottom of the lake and would in time push the water out of the mud to give a reasonable foundation.

When all these operations were completed, said Mr Wright, residents' children would be permitted to paddle in the lake at their own risk."

Then in the early 1960s the following article appeared in the same newspaper:

Storm over site with a 600-year history

"The fate of Blendon Lake, Bexley, will be decided in the next few months. The lake, one of the last survivors of the old Blendon Hall Estate, has once again become the centre of a controversy. Should much-needed houses be built on the site, or should the lake be preserved as a picturesque amenity in a built-up area?

Decline, Fall and Transformation

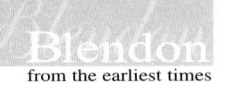

> Residents are determined to save the beauty spot from extinction but Mr. George Wright, the owner, wants to develop the site because he derives no benefit from the lake......
>
> "All I ask at present is outline planning permission for the scheme" says Mr. Wright, of Isfield, Sussex.
>
> Mr. Wright says the majority of the wild ducks came from Danson Park when that lake was drained for widening. He says there are no rhododendrons on his land.
>
> No "sound" trees need felling. Mr. Wright says he consulted the River Board before releasing the water into the stream leading to the River Shuttle."

By the late 1970s, the decision had been made to build on the lake and George Wright saw a return on his investment! But some of the properties needed piles of 30 feet to secure them to a solid foundation!

In the last quarter of the twentieth century, small additions to the estate have been made – the odd house here or there being built into what is a now a thriving residential estate, which along with Penhill, has over 9,000 residents and over 3,500 households.

How can we best summarise the estate? I would invite you to walk round the roads and judge for yourself.

Jim Bowyer's father's vision of an up-market estate is finally complete: spacious plots with individual properties in roads and avenues that rise and fall in sympathy with the contours of the land. Between the houses, glimpses of Repton's trees that 200 years ago would have had their fallen leaves cleared by workers of the Hall and provided shade to the owners.

The West Lodge remains as an office. Jay's Cottages, with their lack of rear windows (to avoid workers gazing at the Hall) still provide shelter, although at today's costs beyond the reach of unskilled labour. Other traces of the Hall lie hidden in private gardens behind walls and fences in this suburban enclave.

Because of the compact habitation, it is difficult, but not impossible, to visualise the Estate as it was. It takes imagination to look up at the Hall from the far side of the lakes on The Drive and understand how the mansion would have dominated the skyline. There is some comfort in knowing, whilst walking up Beechway, that somewhere, not far below your feet, is whatever remains of the pipes and boiler that used to heat the old Georgian home that was once Blendon Hall.

Blendon
from the earliest times

Postscript

Reflections

At the beginning of the twenty-first century how best to reflect on Blendon?

Foremost, Blendon is a living, thriving estate with all the modern facilities and infrastructure that support it. The properties have greatly varying architecture, gardens, outlooks and the estate is home to people of all ages, professions and interests. I believe it remains one of the most attractive places to live – it is not far from its once cherished title of 'second prettiest village in Kent'.

It has a rich history – Royalists, financiers, religious and military men, politicians and bankers – English and American. They have all contributed to the story of Blendon. We must not also forget the most humble child or widow that in some small way contributed to the running of the Estate down the centuries. Blendon was home to all these and more. There were great days;

Fig 96. Top lake - overgrown during the development of the estate

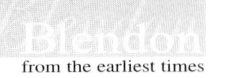

Reflections

Fig 97. Bottom Lake 1950s (Bexley Local Studies)

nineteen year old Frances Dora Smith's wedding to Claude Bowes Lyon in 1853; the celebrations for Edmund Phipps Hornby's triumphant return from the South African War in 1900; there were unusual days – Whitefield's preaching to 3,000 people in 1739 and there were sad days – the premature death of Charles Lambert in 1837 and finally the death of Anna Jay in 1929. And I am sure there must have been many happy days.

More will come to light and a further account of Blendon can be written. Probably best to end now with Whitefield's words, written in June 1739:

"I returned to my sweet retreat at Blendon … It begins our heaven on earth. Were I left to my own choice, here would be my rest."

from the earliest times

Reflections

Fig 98. *The Hall covered with ampelopsis (Virginia creeper) from the west. The driveway gates are open and the single storey building in shade on the right is the conservatory.*
(Bexley Local Studies)

Fig 99. *The Hall from the west in the autumn.* (Bexley Local Studies)

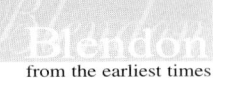

Reflections

Fig 100. The Hall from the west during destruction in 1934 – (Bexley Local Studies)

James Pattison – Commandant of New York 1776

This edited extract from 'The History of the Royal Artillery' – Volume 1 by Captain F Duncan (1872) has been reproduced by kind permission of The Royal Artillery Institution. It describes General James Pattison's time as Commandant of New York in the American War of Independence two years before he purchased the Blendon Estate (see chapter 5).

At the foot of Broadway, in New York (the principal street during the American War) there was a small patch of turf giving its name to the surrounding houses known as the Bowling Green.

Near this Bowling Green lived, during the British occupation in the years 1779 and 1780, James Pattison, Colonel in the Royal Artillery, Major-General in His Majesty's forces in America, and Commandant of the City and Garrisons of New York.

He was the second son of a merchant in London, who owned the Burrage estate at Woolwich and Plumstead. He married a daughter of the celebrated Albert Borgard, and was repeatedly selected for appointments requiring great tact and firmness, two qualities which he possessed in an eminent degree. Among others, he was, as a Lieutenant-Colonel, appointed Lieutenant-Governor of the Royal Military Academy, and did more than any of his predecessors, to introduce a proper discipline among the Cadets and their instructors, while, at the same time, he raised the tone of the institution and asserted its independence of the authorities of the Woolwich garrison.

He served with distinction in Flanders, and at the end of the Seven Years' War he was selected to command the companies selected for service in Portugal. Here he won the respect of all by his dignified firmness and courtesy.

In 1769 Colonel Pattison was sent to Venice to superintend the organisation of the Venetian Artillery. From private letters, still in existence, it would appear that he had a very difficult task with the authorities who were disposed to break faith with him. But as he simply threatened to resign if they did not keep their promises, he obtained what he wanted; and he never wanted more than justice.

General Pattison, succeeded Colonel Cleaveland in the command of the Fourth Battalion of the Royal Artillery in America. He succeeded one who was a soldier, but no statesman. General Pattison was equally sensible of his duty as far as military operations were concerned; but he went beyond his predecessor in the

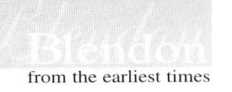

Appendix I

liberal and statesmanlike views he took of the state of America. In his official reports he did not enter into details beyond his province; but his private correspondence is a mine of wealth to the student of the great American War. The following letter is a valuable contribution to the history of those times, and reveals at once the able character of the writer and the state of the American Colonies. In writing to his brother from Philadelphia, in December 1777, he says:

> "I wish it was in my power to give you very pleasing accounts of the state of affairs in this distracted country. Ministers have been deceived, and have never known the true state of this country; if they had, they never would have entered into a war with it. I had very mistaken notions myself when in England of reducing America to obedience by conquest. I have totally changed my sentiments, not that I would wish them to be known but to yourself; but I will confess to you that I am fully of the opinion that all the efforts Great Britain can make will never effectually conquer this great continent. We have not only armies to combat with, but a whole country where every man, woman, and even child is your enemy. One Royal Army has been already obliged to lay down their arms, and surrender prisoners of war; another army at New York in a state of alarm; and the Grand Army here penned up within the narrow limits of two or three miles. In short, unless thirty thousand men more, added to the thirty thousand we already have, can be sent hither early in the year, the wisest thing would be to get rid of the contest in the best manner you can, and, if it was possible to persuade them to revoke their Declaration of Independence, then to make one general Act of Oblivion – give up entirely the point of taxation, and restore the whole country to the state it was in 1763. These are my politics, though I would not wish them to be known. I am much afraid the prosecution of the war must prove ruinous and destructive to Great Britain."

These words have a special value, coming from one whose official position in command of the Artillery gave him favourable opportunities for forming an opinion. Opinions never interfered with the performances of duties, however hopeless; and no one was more energetic than General Pattison, both at Philadelphia and in his command at New York. We learn from this letter three things – the success of the cry against England commenced in Massachusetts, and swollen by hasty and foolish treatment on the part of England; the falsehood of the Government statements at home; and the great difficulties which embarrassed the English Army in its operations, even early in the war.

But in this chapter the condition of New York during the British occupation is the subject of consideration; and, perhaps, it cannot be better realised than by imagining oneself in the company of the gallant General, as he went his daily rounds.

We are at No. 1 Broadway, on the Bowling Green, where the General lives. His chestnut horse is at the door, and Captain Adye and Captain-Lieutenant Ford, his Quartermaster, are waiting for him.

The General is a wiry, muscular man, of about fifty-four years of age: – his staff were mere boys, and yet he outlived them both. The characteristic which struck

Appendix I

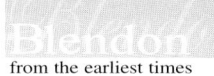

every one most was his courtly urbanity: every hat which was raised by passers-by was courteously acknowledged: and for every one whom he knew there was a pleasant, kindly word.

The General was, in the strongest and most benevolent sense, a father to his officers, there was no one in whose affairs he was not ready to take an interest; and his sympathy with all under his command is visible in every line of his correspondence. As the student sits among his letter-books, in the Dryasdust Record Office looking out on the Thames, out of the yellow pages and faded writing, there seems to shape itself a figure, which has such a loveable reality about it. In return for the interest the General felt in and showed for his officers, he asked but one thing – their confidence.

There is a letter which the General had written to a friend at Woolwich, who superintended the recruiting from the Battalion, which was then much below its establishment. In answer to repeated remonstrances, a few handfuls of men from the other Battalions were sent, – not the best. At last, recruits being no longer obtainable in England, the experiment was tried of recruiting in Ireland, and the first draft was sent to the 4th Battalion. At this time the Irish Artillery, afterwards the 7th Battalion of the Royal Artillery, secured the best recruits in Ireland. The refuse only remained for the Royal Artillery, and the following is the graphic language used by the General in describing the new levies as they landed in New York.

> "The drafts have arrived, four having deserted, and one died upon the passage. I should not have been very much afflicted if many of those who landed here had saved me, either by death or desertion, the pain of looking at them, for such warriors of 5 feet 5 inches I never saw raised before for the service of Artillery."
>
> "Hard times, indeed, and great must be the scarcity of men when the Royal Artillery is obliged to take such reptiles. I would they were back in the bogs from which they sprang."

The last letter to be quoted is a more serious one; and is addressed to the Right Honourable the Board of Ordnance, at this time very wooden-headed, very obstinate, very devoted to every form of circumlocution.

> Their officials loved then to snub, and carp, and disallow; and to look with suspicion on any one who dared to think for himself. The officials of the Ordnance have passed away; but who shall say that the type is extinct?
>
> Ah! this gunner who governed New York! He had his rough hours with the rebels and with the citizens, and with his motley army, but the roughest were when the convoys coming in brought the usual budget of stupendous idiocy, written by clerks who knew not, probably, whether America lay to the east or the west of the Tower, but who felt that their duty was to be to the conscientious officer an eternal nightmare.

Before doing anything else, the General's custom during his morning's ride was to look at the batteries near his house, known then as Fort George and Grand Battery. The former was a regular fortification, and the latter mounted 94 guns. They

Appendix I

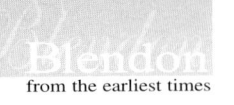

commanded the river between New York and Brooklyn heights, and New York and Staten Island. The fortifications on Brooklyn heights, especially Fort Stirling, had been immensely strengthened by General Pattison, and not a point on New York Island was left unarmed by him. He availed himself of many breast-works and trenches, and of large works like Fort Independence, and he strengthened them in the most laborious and efficient manner. To his efforts more than any other's, was the fact due that the City remained unmolested during the whole war. His labours and duties were enormous. His command being co-extensive with the North American continent, he would one day receive demands for powder and guns from Halifax, Nova Scotia, and the next day from Florida, or from Captain Traille in Virginia.

The reader will now be good enough to accompany the General up Broadway, towards Hester Street, in the Bowery, then one of the extreme streets yet built in New York, and near the spot where the British landed on 16 September, 1776, to occupy the city. It was close to the place where St Mark's Church now stands. In Hester Street lived Mrs Douglas, the young wife of as brave a subaltern of Artillery as every stepped. The General had just received a despatch from Sir Henry Clinton, then engaged in operations up the Hudson, in which young Douglas's bravery, coolness, and skill had been mentioned in the highest terms. Before writing to his subaltern to express the satisfaction he derived from such a report, the General hastened to tell the good news to Mrs Douglas, for it enabled him to add to his letter a postscript which he knew young Douglas would value, giving all the latest news from his home. It was this thoughtfulness which endeared him to his officer. The day shall come when the General shall stop in the same street at a door not much farther on, but his face shall be sad, and his step slow, as he mounts the staircase to tell of a young husband lying under the turf near Charlestown, wounded to death in the battle, and dying with his wife's name on his lips, and love for her in his glazing eye. As he enters the room, there shall be that in his face which a woman's wit shall too quickly read, and the cry of a broken heart shall echo on the old man's ears for years to come!

Leaving Hester Street the General rode towards Ranelagh House, then a species of Tea Gardens, out of the city, but only a little east of the present intersection of Anthony Street and West Broadway.

In continuing his ride, the General went to Greenwich, a village situated at that time a mile and a half out of the city, but now in the very heart of it, where the German troops in English pay were stationed, Of all the mistakes made by England in that war – and they were many – the hiring of mercenaries to fight the Americans was perhaps the greatest. It irritated many loyal men into rebellions, and gave a union and cohesion to the disloyal, such as they never otherwise would have gained. Nor were the mercenaries very valuable as soldiers; they were

Appendix I

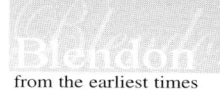

discontented and quarrelsome. Apart, however, from the general question, there was no Commanding officer whose management of the foreign troops displayed so much tact, as General Pattison. Whether it were on duty, or on such occasions as the celebrated ball given by him on the King's Birthday in 1780, which he opened with the wife of the German Baron who commanded at Greenwich, his courtesy and tact were always exerted to cement differences, or allay grievances.

Returning homewards from Greenwich, the General rode through a great many burnt streets, burnt by incendiaries the night after the English occupied New York, and at a fire which took place later; – past not a few churches which had been converted into prisons, riding-schools, and hospitals, for at times the sickness in the city was very great; – past Vauxhall, where Sir Peter Warren lived; past the house in Hanover Square where Prince William stayed, when set out by the King in compliment to his American subjects, and past the dwelling of Admiral Walton. As he rode along, he passed printed anathemas on the walls against privateering, and notices of 20 guineas reward from the Government, and 10 guineas additional from the insurance offices, for the discovery of any man who should have seduced a soldier on board a privateer. There were no less than 5000 New Yorkers engaged during the war in this lawless occupation. It was certainly adding insult to injury, after the sleepless nights they sometimes caused to the General, but the owners of a very fast privateer had actually the impertinence to name their ship after him.

On his way home he rode into the Ordinance Yard, where a few words of comfort had to be spoken to the men whose wages were so disproportionate to those of ordinary civil labourers, that not merely were they discontented, but they could hardly live at all.

The General having now returned to Broadway, let two or three instances be mentioned, in which he prominently figured during his command at New York, before closing this chapter.

The first shall be the only instance in which the General ever showed any symptom of insubordination. He forgot the soldier is the gunner. On the last day of May, 1779, he accompanied Sir Henry Clinton, the Commander-in-Chief, to within 3 miles of Stony Point on the Hudson, and as Artillery became necessary in carrying out the proposed attack, General Pattison was ordered to take command of the troops. During the dark, moonless night – the Artillery for the service was got up, and the batteries completed by five o'clock in the morning, notwithstanding great difficulties, arising from a bad landing-place and a very steep precipice.

Orders were then given to commence firing on the enemy's works, and, notwithstanding the great distance, the fire was soon seen to have been effectual. Sir Henry

Appendix I

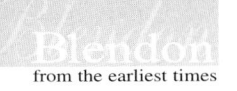

Clinton therefore sent instructions to the General to cease firing, but the General's blood was up. The range had been got to an inch, and so instead of ceasing fire, he sent back an earnest request to be allowed a few more rounds. Very soon, however, a white flag was seen; and in a few minutes it was known that the whole rebel force had surrendered.

The next sketch may be said to show the culminating point of the General's career as Commandant of New York. The winter of 1779 was the hardest, it is believed, ever recorded in that city. The water was frozen between New York and Staten Island, and guns were carried over on sleighs. It was an anxious time. The insular advantages of New York disappeared before this unexpected high-road of ice; the Jerseys were swarming with Washington's troops; and as nearly the whole of the regular forces had gone from New York to Charlestown on special service, the General dreaded an attack which he might be unable to resist. Notwithstanding the croaking of many advisers, he resolved to arm the inhabitants, to test the sincerity of their professions of loyalty, and to ascertain whether his rule in the city had been a successful one.

And the event proved that he was right. In a few hours he had 4,300 loyal volunteers between 17 and 60 years of age, armed at their own expense, until arms could no longer be brought, when they received them from the King's stores; he had merchants of the city standing sentry on his own house; and so fired was the Admiral by his energy, that he landed all the sailors he could spare, and put them under his orders.

The anxiety the General suffered during the winter of 1779 aggravated a complaint from which he had been suffering for some time, which he describes in his diary as "a stubborn disease which no medicine can cure", and he began to feel that rest and change were necessary. So he applied for, and obtained, leave of absence to go home for the benefit of the Bath waters; but so reluctant was he to leave his post that it was late in the autumn of 1780 before he actually did. During the three years of his command he had got everything into such admirable order, that its transfer to his successor was simpler than could have been expected from its complicated and extensive nature. He received a perfect ovation on his departure, both from the civil and military part of the population; and the dear old man had hardly set down in Bath, before he wrote off to all his old friends of the 4th Battalion.

In all that General Pattison did – whether on duty or not – he was essentially conscientious and hard-working. A brief notice of his death will suitably close this chapter. He lived to be a very old man. Twice he was appointed Commandant of Woolwich, a command less onerous than that which he held in America, but still a prize to which every Artillery officer looks forward. At last, on a wild March morning in the year 1805, death stole into Hill Street, Berkeley Square, and touched on the shoulder, in his 82nd year, the gallant old soldier.

Garden Life Article 1903

GARDEN LIFE
(ILLUSTRATED)
A Practical Journal for Amateur Gardeners.

Vol V.   Saturday, December 12, 1903.   No 115

BLENDON HALL, BEXLEY, KENT.

FAMOUS GARDENERS AT HOME

No 114 – Mr W E Humphreys at the Gardens, Blendon Hall, Bexley, Kent

It was the privilege of Mr Humphreys to fill for several years the post of head gardener to Dr Smee, of Carshalton, son of the famous author of "My Garden". As this delightful book indicates, "My Garden" was a most interesting place, almost everything being done in an experimental way, either to find out something fresh, or to prove or disprove fresh theories of Dr Smee's own, or those of other people. The collection of Orchids, especially of Cattleyas, was very fine, and there were eight hundred varieties of Apples and Pears. The rare and curious in plant life always attracted Dr Smee's attention, and, as Mr Humphreys himself said, when I saw him, the other day, at Blendon Hall Gardens, with the courteous assent of Mrs Jay, the owner, "How could I help being benefited by being always connected with this sort of thing?" The relations between the two men were not those of an ordinary employer and gardener, and it is the interesting testimony of Mr Humphreys that Dr Smee told him many things about gardening not generally known, and taught him how to pursue inquiries on scientific lines.

"And how long have you been at Blendon Hall", I inquired, as we started for a stroll round the houses and gardens attached to one of the most charming mansions in Kent. "I succeeded the late Mr Moore, who had been here for thirty-three years, twelve months ago, and I felt that, though taking a very onerous post, I was fairly equipped with all-round knowledge. At one time I was in danger of becoming a specialist, but wider experience proved to me the advantage of knowing something of a great variety of subjects."

"I should be glad if you would tell me something of your career before you went to Carshalton?"

"Not liking engineering, for which I was intended, I was apprenticed to gardening, at Firley Park Gardens, Sussex. I left there for Handcross Park, where I worked one year in the Forest and Pinetum, and three years among a grand collection of specimen exhibition plants, first under Mr Charles Rann, and subsequently under Mr Offer. Then I had a short spell at Malvern House, Sydenham, among economic plants, subsequently acting as foreman for two years at Elmstead, Streatham, among Orchids and furnishing plants; and, before I went to 'My Garden' as foreman, under Mr G W Cummins, I spent some time in Messrs Sanders' establishment at St Albans."

"Were you foreman at Dr Smee's for a considerable period?"

"For eight years. When Mr Cummins left, I became head and continued to fill that post until the death of Dr Smee."

"I gather that now you have no special love of any particular class or part of gardening?"

"That is so; but I am very fond of hardy fruit growing, herbaceous plants, and vegetables. Exhibiting I am not fond of, though I have staged exhibits from all parts of the garden,

Appendix II – Garden Life Article 1903

MR. W. E. HUMPHREYS

and table decorations. But, beyond a certificate or two, and one or two medals, I have nothing to show for a great deal of effort. At Blendon I find that quality is the chief consideration, though quantity is also important as for nine or ten months in the year the family are in residence, and, while only three in number, visitors are numerous."

"What is the extent of the park and gardens?"

"The park is ninety acres, and the estate one hundred and twenty. We employ from fourteen to fifteen men in the gardens, some of whom are housed in the bothy. In addition to the gardens here, I have charge of the estate."

Here we paused where potting operations were progressing, and Mr Humphreys said:-

"We grow about five hundred Strawberry plants, all Royal Sovereign, which, I think, is at once the best early and the best late forcing variety."

"Violets, I see you go in for considerably?"

"Yes; our chief wants are something to cut, something to look at, and something to eat; and anything useful in either of these directions has every care and attention. We are giving up The Czar, and almost confining ourselves to the Princess of Wales, because of the length of the stem and the superiority of the colour. Also the Princess of Wales is the best spring-growing Violet. We make rather a feature of the Polyanthus."

"Which do you consider the finest strain?"

"I get the seed from William Laing, of Sutton. We always sow the Polyanthus in autumn, instead of in spring, and we have flowers more or less all through the winter. It is true that sowing in August means that it takes sixteen months to get flowers, instead of twelve. But by this system we get much finer plants, and they are more established to make big spikes of flowers. I adopted it originally because the Polyanthus germinates better in the autumn than in the spring. The dark varieties are the best in this strain. My own opinion is that there is not enough made of the Polyanthus. We have between five and six hundred plants, and get a big patch of colour in the spring."

Entering the houses devoted to Melons, Cucumbers, and Tomatoes, in the summer, I noticed a quantity of Primulas, and Mr Humphreys remarked:-

"We grow the Primula that stings – P obconica; but none of our people have been stung by it, and it is a very useful plant. We used to have one colour only, but now there are different shades of the same variety. The other varieties of Primula grown are P.alba plena, Williams' single mixed, and Stellata, which is known, because of its gracefulness, as the Lady Primula. We grow about two hundred Primulas. All our table plants, as you will perceive, are in bowl-shaped pans. This is done in order to keep them as dwarf as possible, as we are limited to a height of nine or ten inches."

"Like a good many others, you grow Humea elegans?"

"It has become popular again during the last three or four years. I once showed eight plants of Humea elegans, fourteen feet high, the stems being clothed down to the ground. They were grown almost in a cool house. A temperature of fifty degrees in the winter is plenty for them, but they must not be stinted for pot-room. These large plants were finished in 14-in. pots."

"How many Poinsettias do you grow?"

"Between a hundred and fifty and two hundred. We depend upon Poinsettias for colour at Christmas, but not upon young plants only. Half of our collection are saved from last year. Poinsettias are not difficult to grow, if they are neither over-fed nor over-watered. Our variety is pulcherrima."

"And your variety of Amarylis?"

"Reticulata. We grow about fifty of these. Some have thrown up four spikes from a bulb, each spike carrying eight flowers. As some of the posts have three or four bulbs in, they are a grand sight. I do not know of anything to beat Amaryllis reticulata in the bulb line, during September, October, and November. Our treatment is to pot them in February, and grow them until they have finished flowering, in November. Then we rest them till February again. We have had some four hundred flowers from our plants this year. I fancy that the variety is rather scarce"

"Which variety of Begonia Gloire de

AN EFFECTIVE GROUP OF CAMPANULA PRYAMIDALIS.

Appendix II – Garden Life Article 1903

Lorraine do you prefer?"

"I like the pink better than the white. We grow about two hundred pots. Also we have Begonia Haageana and Madame Carnot. The former, with its pink buds among the whitish flowers, is a very striking plant. We grow about twenty-five varieties of Zonal Pelargoniums, in thirty-two pots – a hundred in all. The best varieties are Improved Raspail (a good double scarlet), Lady Curzon (pink), Snowstorm (snow-white), Golden Rain (Indian red), Ben Hope (pink and white), Mary Pelton (very pale pink), Coronation (scarlet and white centre)."

Passing through the kitchen garden, I observed a collection of Cactus Dahlias, and Mr Humphreys said:-

"We grow the green Dahlia, Viriditflora. It throws up, occasionally, a crimson petal. Other varieties are Hohenzollern (the best buff), Mrs Crowe (yellow), Red Rover (scarlet), Lord Brassey (pink), and Lord Roberts (white). Lord Roberts is very free-flowering, and whiter than any of the other whites."

"You use the Vineries for Chrysanthemums?"

"At present, and then, when the Vines are started, for forcing all the spring-flowering plants. We grow about a thousand Chrysanthemums, including, of decorative varieties, fifty bushes of W H Lincoln, fifty of Mrs Filkins, fifty of Souvenir d'une Petit Amie, fifty of Mary Anderson (the best white to stand up well), and fifty of Ryecroft Glory. Of the Japanese and Incurved, the bronzes and the yellows are the most useful. Freesias have just come into this house. We keep them out through October. There are about a thousand bulbs. Also in here, for bedding, are about two thousand Geraniums. We try to arrange, when bedding out, so that there are pinks on one side of the house and scarlets on the other, so that both colours cannot be seen at the same time."

"What Grapes do you go in for, chiefly?"

"Alicantes, Muscats, and Black Hamburghs."

"You have two remarkable Fig trees?"

"These two trees have given us a thousand fruit. St John's fruits in July, and Negro Largo in September. The latter is a very good variety. The trees have been in this mixed house for seven or eight years. They are not trained, but open out. Originally, they were in pots, and they were planted here on a mound of brick. It is necessary to dig a trench round the base of the bricks every year, to check exuberant growth, and put a little mortar-rubbish in the trench."

In the early Peach house were a number of Pompon and single Chrysanthemums, and Mr Humphreys expressed his regret that Pompons seem to be going out of fashion. In one of the greenhouses there were about two hundred Carnations (Marguerite), and a number of the Tree varieties. I asked which were the best of the Tree.

"The American Tree Carnation have more constitution than any other, and three best of the American varieties are President Roosevelt, Queen Louise, and Mrs T W Lawson."

"Nasturtiums," continued Mr Humphreys, "grow on the roof. Spitfire is an exceptionally good climber. We cut quantities of the flower; the colour is very good, and they are very welcome occasionally for the table in winter. In the stove we have about forty plants of Calanthe Veitchii, which I hope to increase to a hundred. Euphorbia jacquiniæflora, with Crotons, Dracænas, and small Palms, among the other contents of the stove."

"You have more than one herbaceous border, I observe?"

"Yes; we have one about a hundred yards by fourteen, and another, in front of the house, eighty by five. You see that we have some Iris stylosa. It thrives in mild weather in winter, and a little touch of blue at this season of the year in the pleasure grounds is very acceptable. This Iris Mrs Jay saw in Germany last winter, and liked it so much that I procured a few."

"Which species of shrubs do you find flourish most?"

"Hollies and Laurels. There are a number of big trees of great age in the park, including Sweet Chestnuts, Elms, and Oaks."

"When was the house erected?"

"The original mansion was built about four hundred years ago, and I suppose that the gardens date from that time. The Ampelopsis Veitchii, on the west front, and the Wistaria sinensis on the south front of the house, are very fine. The French Honeysuckle also grows on the walls."

"You have a wide expanse of lawn, and plenty of water?"

"The undulating lawns are four acres in extent, and there are four lakes. We have only the common yellow Lily in the water. It is indigenous. I am trying to get rid of it, in order to make room for good varieties. But, so long as the yellow Lily remains, it is useless to try to grow others."

In the conservatory the feature is a circular ladder stage at the end, and I congratulated Mr Humphreys upon its imposing appearance.

"That stage has always to be filled," he rejoined. "It is now entirely occupied by the Chrysanthemum Mary Anderson, and its yellow sport, Miss Annie Holden. The latter is not known, much yet, but the white and yellow – from fifty to sixty bushes – make a fine mixture of colour. In addition to the contents of the conservatory, there are about a hundred and twenty plants in the hall; also the numerous vases outside have to be filled."

"What are your usual spring-bedding plants?"

"Yellow Alyssums, white Arabis, pink Silenes, and Forget-me-nots, all bedded under Tulips of the shades that suit the flowers. There are also two large beds of Wallflowers, containing about nine hundred plants. The varieties are Belvoir Castle and Vulcan, Rhododendrons, by the way, grow here without artificial aid. The loamy soil, which is absolutely without lime, suits them."

"Then you have a sub-tropical bed. What do you grow in it?"

"Solanum Ralbisii, mixed with Perilla Nankinensis. The former has a good flower attached to it. Here we have also Castor-oil plants, various Solanums, Nicotianas, and Cannas."

"We have not said anything about Roses and Border Carnations."

"Roses are quite a feature. We are introducing Hybrid Teas in preference to Hybrid Perpetuals, for continuous flowering. Ramblers will be planted in all directions on old trees, etc. We have about a thousand plants of Border Carnations in seven or eight varieties only."

Among other features is a north avenue of Limes, planted nearly two hundred years ago, and the autumn tints of a fine collection of Axalea rustica, seven or eight feet high, caught my fancy.

"My efforts here," observed Mr Humphreys, "are highly appreciated, and work is made most pleasant for me. Mrs Jay is fond of all flowers, but her own particular little garden she likes best to have full of Daffodils land grass, hedged in with Sweet Brier."

"Now, as to the features of the kitchen garden.".

"First, I should explain that we are fortunate in having a ploughed field for Potatoes, Cauliflowers, and Broccoli. The latter, especially, do much better than in a garden, owing to more air. As to the kitchen garden proper, we go in for everything that can be used for salads, even for Dandelions. Lettuces are cut every day in the year, a great deal by the aid of frames and shelters. The chief variety is All the Year Round. Of Celery, I prefer Veitch's Solid White. For summer salads we grow Rampion, an Austrian form of Cress. We have also the Italian Corn salad, and Chives, a mild kind of Garlic. Maize is largely grown as a vegetable, the seed always being procured from America."

"I suppose that you had a poor crop of Apples and Pears?"

"The Pears were very thin, but the Apple crop was quite up to the average. I attribute our good fortune to shelter afforded to the trees when they were in bloom. Our best varieties include Bramley's Seedling. Peasgood's Non-such, King of Pippins, Warner's King, Ecklinville Seeding, Blenheim, Orange, King Pippin, and Baunabb's Red Winter Russet, the best all-round Apple."

"How were your other crops in the kitchen garden?"

"Strawberries and Gooseberries were fair, but the frost cut the Black and Red Currants when they were in bloom. Of Peas we had an astonishing crop, and were picking in November. Among other varieties grown are Gradus and English Wonder. We picked a nice dish of Runner Beans on November 13th. The variety is Sutton's Prize Winner."

"Have you, in spite of your responsibilities here, any time to spare for outside work?"

"I join in discussions at the meetings of gardeners' mutual societies, and have read papers. My idea is that such gatherings do a lot of good. I thoroughly believe in ventilating questions of interest and importance to those employed in horticulture. Finally, I may say, as to systems, that there is no straight line to follow. Adaptability to circumstances ensures success."

ALFRED WILCOX

Wedding Report – Bexleyheath Observer 1910

WEDDING AT BEXLEY.

Rodwell-Jay.

Quite an epidemic of military marriages has been experienced recently and the number was added to yesterday (Thursday) by the celebration of the nuptials of Miss Sophie Jay, daughter of the late Mr Carl Jay, and Mrs Carl Jay, of Blendon Hall, Bexley, and granddaughter of the late Mr William C Pickersgill, and Lieut-Col R M Rodwell, R H A., youngest son of the late Mr Edgar Rodwell, KC. The bride's family has been associated with the Bexley district for nearly half a century, and as its various members have always taken a deep interest in the welfare of those around them, it was not surprising to find that all classes of the community evinced an active interest in such a happy event. The ceremony took place at Bexley parish church where the bride's mother was married forty years since by the Rev T Harding. The sacred edifice was profusely adorned with palms and flowering and foliage plants, under the direction of Mr W E Humphreys, head gardener, and was well filled when the bridal party arrived, whilst hundreds of spectators unable to obtain admission to the church formed up on either side of the path leading to the main entrance. The bride, escorted by her brother, Mr William C P Jay, was attired in white satin with old Brussels lace, the gift of her mother, and wore a tulle veil, a wreath of natural orange blossoms, and a diamond pendant, the gift of her mother. The bridal bouquet was the handiwork of Mr Humphreys, and was much admired for its artistic arrangement. The bridesmaids were Misses Valerie and Nora Jay, Misses Irene and Betty Phipps Hornby (nieces of the bride), Misses Nancy and Hilda Rodwell (nieces of the bridegroom). Their dresses were composed of spotted muslin. They also wore Dutch lace caps, and carried crooks, with bouquets of pink carnations, which with diamond and pearl wreath brooches were the gifts of the bridegroom. They presented quite a picture as they formed up in a triangle in the aisle. Lieutenant-Colonel Rodwell was accompanied by Major C van Straubenzee, R.F.A., as best man. The officiating clergy were the Rev J H Wicksteed, vicar of Bexley, and the Rev M M Cassidy, vicar of St James', Westgate. Mr Harold Moore presided at the organ, and played extempore during the time the congregation was assembling. The processional hymn was "O Father all creating," and that at the close of the service "O perfect love, all human thought transcending." Whilst the newly married couple walked to the vestry the "Wedding March" from Lohengrin pealed through the old church, and as the procession returned Mendlessohn's "Wedding March" was played. A number of school children lined the avenue from the church to the lych gate, and bestrewed the path of the bridal couple with rose leaves. The weather was all that could be desired for the occasion, the sun's rays being tempered by a cooling westerly breeze, and this enabled the fair sex, who formed the larger part of the congregation, to display the latest confections in rich profusion. At the conclusion of the ceremony the wedding party returned to Blendon Hall, where a reception was held, and was attended by about 200 guests. The band of the Royal Artillery played during the afternoon, and the spacious suite of reception rooms on the ground floor, giving access to the lawn at the rear of the house, were all decorated with choice flowers from the gardens and greenhouses.

The presents numbering 350, were arranged in the library, and were greatly admired. Not the least appreciated of the souvenirs were those sent by the domestic staff (a handsome silver bowl) the outside staff (salad bowl) women and children of the village (siphon holder), Bridgen women (jam pot), and teachers and children of Bridgen schools, (salt cellars).

The newly-married couple left during the afternoon en route for Scotland. The bride's travelling dress was of Nattier blue charmeuse, and black tulle hat.

LIST OF PRESENTS.
Col and Mrs E Percival, lace collar.
Major and Hon Mrs Dennis, bridge case
Mrs W Jay, print.
Mrs Dwight Collier, silver coffee set.
Mr and Mrs T Ingham, china tea set.
Mrs Mayne, fan.
Mrs and Miss Blake, silver sugar bowl.
Mr and Mrs Passavant, kettle.
Mr and Mrs Ingham Whitaker, plated silver sauce boats.
Mrs Arbuvinne, Venetian lace sofa back.
Rev H and Mrs Shepherd, pair silver spoons.
Mr and Mrs A Schlesinger, empire cloak.
Mr and Mrs Arthur Whitaker, dessert set.
Mr and Mrs Barton, silver tea caddy.
Mr A Gille, dressing case.
Sir John and Lady Rodger, Gold hat pins.
Capt and Mrs G Phipps Hornby, silver match box.
Mr R Cooper, antique caddy.
Major and Mrs Talbot, pair Sheffield candlesticks.
Mrs Cubitt, sugar scoop.
Miss Noble Taylor, hat-pin stand.
Major and Mrs Ferrar, breakfast set.
Major and Mrs Hope Johnstone, dessert service.
Mrs H Schlesinger, pin cushion.
Miss Outhwaite, cheque.
Col and Mrs Vores, tallboy.
Mrs Joshua Fielden, Russian necklet.
The Mrs Pickersgill Cunliffe, large Turkey carpet.
Household servants of Blendon Hall, large silver bowl.
Tommy and Bobby Evans, silver menu holders.
Capt and Mrs Trandy, lace fan.
Mr and Mrs C Pilkington, 8 silver vases.
Gardeners and Men of Blendon, salad bowl.
Women and children of Blendon, syphon stand.
Rev P Egerton, silver ink stand and tray.
Col R M Rodwell, furs (muff and boa).
Mrs Pickersgill Cunliffe, travelling cushion.
Mr R Arbuthnot, pair Sheffield dishes.
Rev R Dale, prayer and hymn book.
Sir Walter Armstrong, silver hand glass.
The Misses Evans, Sheffield candelabra.
Miss F Evans, gold and coral chain.
Miss Helen Arbuthnot, sweet basket.
Mr Clinton Dent, pair silver sauce cellars.
Mr J T Johnson, silver calendar.
Capt and Mrs R Phipps Hornby, gold purse.
H B and A Borgnis, revolving bookcase.
Mr F G Arbuthnot, cake stand.
Mrs Borgnis, despatch box.
Capt and Mrs Rennie, silver hand glass.
Mr Trapmann, bridge table and box.
Sir G and Lady Molesworth, silver sweet dishes.
Miss K Edwards, silver looking glass.
Miss Moorhouse, hat pins.
Mrs Spencer, trinket box.
Mr and Mrs Bowman, butter dish.
Major and Mrs Rouse, china bowls.
The Misses Fielden, silver sauce boats.
Mr G Evans, pearl and sapphire pendant.
Miss Clara Heinemann, silver posset dish.
Mr and Mrs Pickersgill Cunliffe, thermos case.
Miss Cameron and Miss Munro, Chippendale chair.
The Misses Kinder, silver ink pot.
Mr and Mrs A Goldschmidt, enamelled bell push.
Mr Robert Gordon, silver candlesticks.
Mr and Mrs C H Gray, silver candlestick.
Mrs Thompson, teachers and Bridgen school children, 4 silver salt cellars.
Mr and Mrs L Kekewich, gold bracelet.
Major and Mrs Cruikshank, magnifying glass.
Mr A H Trevor, coffee machine, tray, etc.
Women of Bridgen, jam pot.
Miss and Mr J Grant, silver candlesticks.
Miss Friend, toby jug.
Mr and Mrs G de Geofray, buckle.
Dr and Mrs Hinds, silver frame.
Mrs Wilson, pair of glass vases.
Mr T Lodge, silver bowl.
Captain and Mrs Foster, antique liqueur glasses.
Mrs Horner, sugar sifter.
Miss M Horner, cushion.

Appendix III – Wedding Report – Bexleyheath Observer 1910

Mr and Mrs R Ferard, glass bowls.
Mr and Mrs Vesey Holt, coffee cups and saucers.
Mrs S C Jay, cheque.
Irene and Betty Phipps Hornby, gate table.
Mr R Jones, china vases.
Gen Buston CB and Gen Lawson CB, silver potato ring.
Col and Mrs Herbert, "Tortoise" bell.
Miss Byren, Tortoiseshell box.
Gen Mrs and the Misses Hayward, "Sluggards Delight".
Major A Young RHA, glass decanter.
Rev J H and Mrs Wicksteed, silver vase.
Mr and Mrs Bliss, silver cream jug.
Miss Vores, Norwegian spoons.
Miss Tyler, blotter.
Mrs Carl Jay, diamond pendant, diamond necklet, household linen, fur coat.
Mr and Mrs and Miss Elgood, silver bowl.
Mrs Ireland, purse and opera glasses.
Capt Livingstone Learmouth RHA, china box.
Mr and Mrs Anstruther, silver muffineers.
Dr J E Walker, silver vases.
Mr and Mrs John Grant, picture.
Mr and Mrs F Jay, gold spoons etc.
Mr and Mrs Keep, silver pheasant.
Mr and Mrs A Ferard, muffin dish.
Miss Fraser, storm kettle.
Mr and Mrs M von Metzler, cushion.
General L B Friend CB, silver bowl.
Miss Bevers, D'oylies.
Rev and Mrs B Davies, brass knockers.
Mr and Mrs Liebenrood, scent bottles.
Mr and Mrs B Wilkinson, antique sauce boat.
Major and Mrs Robinson, table.
Mrs C. Birch, scent bottle.
Mrs Bean, silver salver.
The Misses Bean, Mr L Bean and Mr. and Mrs . F. Kinder, silver cake basket.
Col and Mrs Phipps Hornby, Mr and Mrs William Jay, Miss E Jay, Col and Mrs Pratt, table silver chest.
Mr and Mrs Norsworthy and Miss Russell, card case.
Mrs Stoneham, china vase.
Mr and Mrs E Fielden, silver salver.
Major and Mrs Tinker, Dorothy bag.
Major and Mrs Perkins, Japanese clasp.
Hon Mr and Mrs Marsham Townshend, tea knives.
Miss Nora Jay, picture.
Miss L and Mr J Ferard, coffee cups.
Miss Alice Sargent, pin cushion.
Herr and Frau von Meister, silver fish knives and forks.
Mr Harper, cushion.
Mr and Mrs Otto Hanck, cushion.
Commander and Mrs Bourchier Wrey, bag.
Mr and Mrs W W Mann, coffee and liqueur set.
Mr and Mrs Borton May, scent bottle.
Miss Valerie Jay, napkin rings.

Mrs Walter Heinemam, En-tout-cas.
Misses N and H Rodwell, sugar sifter.
Miss H Munro, handerchief and jacket.
Mr Norrie Sellar, knives.
Mr Louis Jay, carvers.
Mr Leslie and family, silver vases.
Mr and Mrs Foot, tea cloth.
Miss Harris, vase.
Mrs Egerton, embroidery.
Mr and Mrs Beal, flower pot.
Toby and Mimosa, jewel case.
Capt and Mrs Vansittart, magnifying glass.
Miss E Jay, Mrs Christian Jay, Dr and Mrs Jay, Mr and Mrs H Metzier, dessert service, tea and coffee set of Dresden china.
Mrs Trapman, enamelled pendant.
Mr and Mrs Kidd, mustard pot.
Mr J Alera Hankey, clock.
Rev M and Mrs Cassidy, clock.
Mr and Mrs A Shepherd, two chairs.
Major Leslie and Col Hobday, etching and song.

COL RODWELL'S PRESENTS
Officers of the 28th Brigade, RFA revolving breakfast dish and entrée dishes.
Major and Mrs Belfield, cheque.
Mr A Belfield, stick.
Gen Burton CB, cheque.
Major and Mrs Noel Birch, pepper pots.
Mr and Mrs Dugdale, barograph.
Col J Dunlop, decanter.
Col Enthoven RHH, silver dish.
Col and Mrs Finlay, water colour.
Col and Lady Mary Forester Walker, antique chairs.
Mr Hussey and Mr E Hussey, sweet dishes.
Col and Mrs Phipps Hornby, decanter.
Bride to Bridegroom, pearl pin and suit case.
Miss E Jay, writing table.
Mrs Carl Jay, motor coat.
Major J H Leslie, beakers.
Capt and Mrs Mackey, revolving bookcase.
Gen O'Leary, blotter.
Major Peck, travelling clock.
Col and Mrs Purcell, clock.
Gen A Rochfort, salt cellars.
Mrs and Miss Hasell Rodwell, gravy spoons.
Mr and Mrs and Miss Raymond Rodwell, silver dessert knives and forks.
Mr and Mrs H Rodwell, Buhl clock.
Miss Daisy Rodwell, syphon stand.
Miss Hunter Rodwell, sugar tongs.
Mr and Mrs E H Rodwell, dining room clock.
Miss G Hunter Rodwell, silver toast racks.
Capt K Kincard Smith, silver salva.
Col. Slee, cheque.
Capt. Stevenson, mustard pot.
Col. and Mrs. Scott, silver salver.
Capt. Stranack, silver vases.
Capt. Woodroffe, Japanese waistcoat buttons.
Major G. White, gold links.
Mr. and Mrs. F. Anthony White, silver mustard pot.
Mr. E. Wagg, gold pencil case.
Col. Wing, cigarette box.
Rev. L. and Mrs. Lycett, silver.

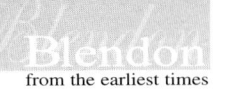

Illustration Acknowledgements

Specific illustration acknowledgements have been given in the text.

I would like to thank the following people who gave permission for photographs of items in their possession to be included in this book.

Geoff Birch; Mrs Boorman and Joan Pollard; Mike and Heather Caley; Mike and Margaret Clinch; Mr and Mrs Cottrell; Peter Hickson; Roy Hopper; Mr and Mrs Huff; Ray Jeal; Mrs Valerie Nicholls; Mrs Pam O'Brien; Mrs Sidgwick; Ray and Ruth Smith; Mrs Dolores Tyers; Rowena Ward-Barrow.

I would also like to thank the following for taking and supplying photographs:

Sue Barclay; Stuart Bligh; Sonia Burns; Mr and Mrs Johnson; Mrs Carol Linaye; Chris Reddall; and Oliver Wooller.

My special thanks to Geoff Holland for all his wizardry in taking, restoring and manipulating photographs.

Finally, a special acknowledgement to the work of Mr A.H.T. Boswell for all his photographs taken in the 1920s and 1930s of Bexley and district, without which so much of our visual history would have been lost.

Places to Go

If you want to find out more about Blendon there are a number of places to go.

Bexley Local Studies and Archive Centre, Central Library, Townley Road, Bexleyheath DA6 7HJ (T: 0208 301 1545 www.bexley.gov.uk)

There are many extra photos of Blendon, which we have not been able to publish in the book and also original documents kept here. If you have any questions about Blendon or wish to give further information contact staff at the centre.

Firepower! The Royal Artillery Museum, The Royal Arsenal, Woolwich SE18 6ST (T: 0208 855 7755 www.firepower.org.uk)

Located at what was the royal artillery site at Woolwich, this modern museum shows the history of ordinance with a combination of audiovisual presentations and exhibits. The collection of weaponry is superb, including tanks and old cannons.

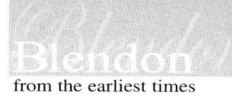

Other References

The links with Blendon are very strong and people who were part of this history are covered together with their medals and other artefacts, including Major Phipps Hornby's Victoria Cross.

The museum is a registered charity.

Weald and Downland Open Air Museum, Singleton, Chichester, West Sussex PO18 0EU (Info. Line: 01243 811348 www.wealddown.co.uk)

Discover a very special place in the heart of the South Downs, an open-air museum where you can explore the homes and gardens, farms and rural workplaces of the past 500 years in South East England.

See traditional farming in action, heavy horses at work, a watermill producing flour and "The Downland Gridshell" – a spectacular new greenoak building to house the Museum's conservation workshop. Dogs on leads and picnickers welcome.

Stately Homes

There are many houses that are open to the public which have features that are similar to Blendon. Especially worth a visit is **Syon Park, Brentford Middlesex TW8 8JF, (T: 0208 569 7497 www.syonpark.co.uk),** the London home of the Duke of Northumberland, has a Gothic façade, a great conservatory and also an icehouse – all features that appeared at Blendon. This is also the location for the film 'Gosforth Park' that featured a country home in the 1930s.

Finally, you can stroll round the Blendon Estate itself and see some of the features referred to in this book. For a short walk (45 minutes) we suggest you start on Blendon Road by the shops, looking at the Lodge and then go down The Drive and walk up Cedar Grove (approximating to the old entrance to the Hall) and then retrace your steps to turn left and continue down The Drive to The Avenue. Turn left here – on either side of the road the lakes were located and the bridge over the channel linking them. Then as you start to climb you come to The Sanctuary where the Hall stood on the north side of this cul-de-sac and on the west side of Beechway. Continue up Beechway and at the top on the left corner stood the other Lodge. Turn left and you are back on Blendon Road with Jay's Cottages on your left.

Footnotes

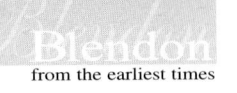

1. Bexley Libraries and Museums - Blendon – 1977 – Ruth Hutcherson
2. Local Studies Notes No. 15 – Blendon - Bexley Local Studies Centre - 1997
3. 'Frogs, Catacombs and Horses' An Illustrated Talk on Blendon Hall and Estate, St James the Great, Blendon, July 1st 2000
4. 'Old spoon could hold the key' News Shopper – Roger Wright – July 19th 2000
5. 'Blendon Hall and Estate' Local History Talk – Hall Place, March 20th 2001
6. 'Heroes and Villains' An Illustrated talk on the history of Blendon Hall St James the Great, Blendon, 28th April 2001
7. Records of D.C. Bowyer and Sons Ltd. BU/DCB /1/3/71 Particulars of Sale of Blendon Hall and Estate 26 November 1863 – Bexley Local Studies Centre
8. 1929 Sales Schedule, Blendon Hall – Bexley Local Studies Centre
9. Ordnance Survey
10. Kentish Times 28th June 1929
11. "Bexleyheath & Welling" Rev. F de P Castell -1910
12. Woolwich Antiquarian Society Volume 14 -1931
13. Medieval Bexley - F R H Du Boulay - 1961
14. Bexley Antiquarian Newsletter 1976 – Ruth Hutcherson
15. Paul Morris Transcripts - Canterbury Assizes 1241 Roll 360, Woolwich and District Antiquarian Society Volume 23 – p 26
16. Bexley Antiquarian Newsletter 1976 – Ruth Hutcherson
17. Medieval Bexley - F R H Du Boulay - 1961
18. Woolwich and District Antiquary Society - W Mandy 1915
19. Records of the Woolwich District Vol. II – W T Vincent 1890
20. Weald and Downland Museum, Singleton, West Sussex
21. The History and Topography of the County of Kent - Edward Hasted 1778
22. Oliver Wooller, Archivist, Bexley Local Studies Centre
23. Bexley. The Church, Hall Place, and Blendon – Canon Scott Robertson 1889
24. Bexley. The Church, Hall Place, and Blendon – Canon Scott Robertson 1889
25. Bexley Libraries and Museums - Blendon – 1977 – Ruth Hutcherson
26. The History and Topography of the County of Kent Edward Hasted 1778
27. Bexley Antiquarian Newsletter 1976 – Ruth Hutcherson
28. Manorial Survey – 1608 - Bexley Local studies Centre
29. Bexley. The Church, Hall Place, and Blendon – Canon Scott Robertson 1889
30. Bexley. The Church, Hall Place, and Blendon – Canon Scott Robertson 1889
31. Bexley Libraries and Museums - Blendon – 1977 – Ruth Hutcherson
32. Burke's Extinct Baronetcies - 1844
33. Bexley Libraries and Museums - Blendon – 1977 – Ruth Hutcherson
34. Rushworth's Historical Coll. Vol. II
35. Officers and Regiments of the Royalist Army 1663
36. English Army Lists and Commission Registers Vol. I – II 1960
37. English Army Lists and Commission Registers Vol. I – II 1960
38. Commissioners for Disbanding the Regiments 1677
39. Bexley Antiquarian Newsletter 1976 – Ruth Hutcherson
40. Bexley. The Church, Hall Place, and Blendon – Canon Scott Robertson 1889
41. A History of Saint Mary's Church Bexley Kent – K M Roome 1974
42. Records of D.C. Bowyer and Sons Ltd. BU/DCB/1/1/17 – Bexley Local Studies Centre
43. Bexley. The Church, Hall Place, and Blendon – Canon Scott Robertson 1889
44. The Great Estates – Oliver Wooller – Bexley Council 2000
45. The Great Estates – Oliver Wooller – Bexley Council 2000
46. Jessica Vale – Museum Collections Manager, Bexley Museum
47. W Brown – Cutlery historian
48. Jessica Vale – Museum Collections Manager, Bexley Museum
49. The History of Parliament – History of Parliament Trust
50. Burkes Landed Gentry 1853
51. The South Sea Bubble – John Carswell – Alan Sutton Publishing 1993

Footnotes

52. The South Sea Bubble – John Carswell – Alan Sutton Publishing 1993
53. The South Sea Bubble – John Carswell – Alan Sutton Publishing 1993
54. The South Sea Bubble – John Carswell – Alan Sutton Publishing 1993
55. The South Sea Bubble – John Carswell – Alan Sutton Publishing 1993
56. The South Sea Bubble – John Carswell – Alan Sutton Publishing 1993
57. The History of Parliament – History of Parliament Trust
58. The South Sea Bubble – John Carswell – Alan Sutton Publishing 1993
59. The South Sea Bubble – John Carswell – Alan Sutton Publishing 1993
60. The South Sea Bubble – John Carswell – Alan Sutton Publishing 1993
61. Burkes Landed Gentry 1852
62. The South Sea Bubble – John Carswell – Alan Sutton Publishing 1993
63. The South Sea Bubble – John Carswell – Alan Sutton Publishing 1993
64. The South Sea Bubble – John Carswell – Alan Sutton Publishing 1993
65. The South Sea Bubble – John Carswell – Alan Sutton Publishing 1993
66. Dictionary of National Biography
67. The Huguenots in England and Ireland, 6th edition - Samuel Smiles 1889
68. George Whitefield – Arnold Dallimore Banner of Truth Trust 1970
69. John Wesley's Journal - 1735
70. Charles Wesley's Journal 1737
71. George Whitefield – Arnold Dallimore Banner of Truth Trust 1970
72. Charles Wesley's Journal 1737
73. Charles Wesley's Journal 1737
74. Charles Wesley's Journal 1737
75. Charles Wesley's Journal 1737
76. George Whitefield – Arnold Dallimore Banner of Truth Trust 1970
77. Whitefield's Journals
78. George Whitefield – Arnold Dallimore Banner of Truth Trust 1970
79. George Whitefield – Arnold Dallimore Banner of Truth Trust 1970
80. George Whitefield Journals
81. George Whitefield Journals
82. George Whitefield – Arnold Dallimore Banner of Truth Trust 1970
83. Whitefield Works Vol.1
84. George Whitefield – Arnold Dallimore Banner of Truth Trust 1970
85. Whitefield Works Vol.1
86. Whitefield Works Vol.1
87. Whitefield Works Vol.1
88. Whitefield Works Vol.1
89. Charles Wesley's Journal 1740
90. Whitefield Works Vol.1
91. Letter from Whitefield to Gilbert Tennent 1740
92. Whitefield Works Vol.2
93. The History and Topography of the County of Kent Edward Hasted 1778
94. The Great Estates Oliver Wooller Bexley Council 2000
95. List of Officers of the Royal Regiment of Artillery, 4th Edition. Royal Artillery Institution 1900
96. Records of D.C. Bowyer and Sons Ltd. BU/DCB/1/2/1 and 1/2/3 – Bexley Local Studies Centre
97. Records of D.C. Bowyer and Sons Ltd. BU/DCB/1/2/6 – Bexley Local Studies Centre
98. The History and Topography of the County of Kent Edward Hasted 1778
99. The History and Topography of the County of Kent Edward Hasted 1778
100. Jim Packer, Local Historian – Transcripts - Land Tax
101. Jim Packer, Local Historian – Transcripts – Window Tax
102. The Great Estates Oliver Wooller Bexley Council 2000
103. A survey of an Estate belonging to the Rt. Honourable Lady Mary Scott and William Scott Esq. at Blenden in the Parish of Bexley in the County of Kent Purchased of Jacob Sawbridge. Centre for Kentish Studies Maidstone Kent

Footnotes

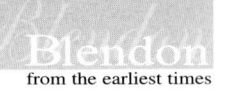

104. Records of D.C. Bowyer and Sons Ltd. BU/DCB/1/2/1 & 1/3/2 – Bexley Local Studies Centre
105. Records of D.C. Bowyer and Sons Ltd. BU/DCB/1/2/8&9 – Bexley Local Studies Centre
106. Records of the Woolwich District – W T Vincent 1890
107. Records of the Woolwich District Vol. II – W T Vincent 1890
108. Records of the Woolwich District Vol. II – W T Vincent 1890
109. List of Officers of the Royal Regiment of Artillery, 4th Edition. Royal Artillery Institution 1900
110. Records of D.C. Bowyer and Sons Ltd. BU/DCB/1/2/14 – Bexley Local Studies Centre
111. Records of D.C. Bowyer and Sons Ltd. BU/DCB/1/3/5 – Bexley Local Studies Centre
112. Records of the Woolwich District – W T Vincent 1890
113. Records of D.C. Bowyer and Sons Ltd. BU/DCB/1/3/15 – Bexley Local Studies Centre
114. 'Smiths the Bankers 1658 –1958' J.A.S.L. Boyce, National Provincial Bank
115. The History of Parliament – History of Parliament Trust
116. The History of Parliament – History of Parliament Trust
117. The History of Parliament – History of Parliament Trust
118. The History of Parliament – History of Parliament Trust
119. Bexley. The Church, Hall Place, and Blendon – Canon Scott Robertson 1889
120. The History of Parliament – History of Parliament Trust
121. Woolwich Antiquarian Society Volume 14 -1931
122. The History of Parliament – History of Parliament Trust
123. The History of Parliament – History of Parliament Trust
124. Biographical Dictionary of Architects - Colvin
125. 'Bexley Mosaic' Workers Educational Association Chapter 2 – Ed Joy Saynor M.A. 1977
126. Biographical Dictionary of Architects - Colvin
127. Fragments on the Theory and Practice of Landscape Gardening – Fragment VIII H Repton and J Adey Repton 1816
128. The History of Parliament – History of Parliament Trust
129. The History of Parliament – History of Parliament Trust
130. The History of Parliament – History of Parliament Trust
131. The History of Parliament – History of Parliament Trust
132. 'Smiths the Bankers 1658 –1958' J.A.S.L. Boyce, National Provincial Bank
133. 'Smiths the Bankers 1658 –1958' J.A.S.L. Boyce, National Provincial Bank
134. Bexley Heath and Welling Rev F de P Castells 1910
135. The Lewin Letters – A Selection from the Correspondence and Diaries of an English Family 1756 – 1884 Volume 1
136. Records of D.C. Bowyer and Sons Ltd. BU/DCB/1/3/29 – Bexley Local Studies Centre
137. 'Smiths the Bankers 1658 –1958' J.A.S.L. Boyce, National Provincial Bank
138. Dictionary of National Biography
139. History of the War in the Peninsula - Napier
140. Dictionary of National Biography
141. Debretts Baronetage of England 1835
142. Records of D.C. Bowyer and Sons Ltd. BU/DCB/1/3/29 – Bexley Local Studies Centre
143. Research Service – Surrey History Centre, Woking
144. Ray Jeal, Local Postal Historian
145. Gentleman's Magazine Part 1 Volume 102 - 1832
146. Ray Jeal, Local Postal Historian
147. Ray Jeal, Local Postal Historian
148, Oliver Wooller, Archivist, Bexley Local Studies Centre
149. Jim Packer, Local Historian
150. Records of D.C. Bowyer and Sons Ltd. BU/DCB/1/3/69 – Bexley Local Studies Centre
151. Ray Jeal, Local Postal Historian
152. Records of D.C. Bowyer and Sons Ltd. BU/DCB/1/3/42 – Bexley Local Studies Centre
153. Group Archives – The Royal Bank of Scotland Group
154. Bexley. The Church, Hall Place, and Blendon – Canon Scott Robertson 1889
155. 'Smiths the Bankers 1658 –1958' J.A.S.L. Boyce, National Provincial Bank
156. 'Smiths the Bankers 1658 –1958' J.A.S.L. Boyce, National Provincial Bank
157. Tithes and Tithe Commutation Act Map – Bexley Local Studies Centre

Footnotes

158. Jim Packer – Local historian
159. Bexley Local Studies Centre
160. Kentish Times April 1937
161. Kentish Times April 1937
162. "Annals of the West Kent Cricket Club" Philip Norman 1897
163. Records of D.C. Bowyer and Sons Ltd. BU/DCB/1/3/48 – Bexley Local Studies Centre
164. Jim Packer, local historian. Transcripts.
165. Group Archives – The Royal Bank of Scotland Group
166. Kentish Times 1937
167. Records of D.C. Bowyer and Sons Ltd. BU/DCB/1/3/71 – Bexley Local Studies Centre
168. Jessica Vale - Museum Collections Manager – Bexley Museum
169. Records of D.C. Bowyer and Sons Ltd. BU/DCB/1/3/71 – Bexley Local Studies Centre
170. Records of D.C. Bowyer and Sons Ltd. BU/DCB/1/3/71 – Bexley Local Studies Centre
171. Kentish Times April 1937
172. Bexley. The Church, Hall Place, and Blendon – Canon Scott Robertson 1889
173. Kentish Times – March 8th 1929
174. Kentish Times – March 8th 1929
175. National Census of Great Britain 1881
176. Kentish Times – March 8th 1929
177. Kentish Times – March 8th 1929
178. St Mary's Church – Bexley
179. 1929 Sales Schedule, Blendon Hall – Bexley Local Studies Centre
180. 1929 Sales Schedule, Blendon Hall – Bexley Local Studies Centre
181. Finance Act Survey – Bexley 1912
182. Garden Life Volume V No 115 December 12 1903 – Interview with W.E. Humphreys
183. National Census of England and Wales 1881
184. Records of D.C. Bowyer and Sons Ltd. BU/DCB/1/3/65 – Bexley Local Studies Centre
185. Records of D.C. Bowyer and Sons Ltd. BU/DCB/1/3/64 – Bexley Local Studies Centre
186. Records of D.C. Bowyer and Sons Ltd. BU/DCB/1/3/65 – Bexley Local Studies Centre
187. Treve Rosoman Curator, English Heritage
188. Bexley Antiquarian Newsletter 1976 – Ruth Hutcherson
189. National Census of England and Wales 1881
190. National Census of England and Wales 1881
191. Records of D.C. Bowyer and Sons Ltd. BU/DCB/1/3/68 – Bexley Local Studies Centre
192. Kentish Times 1925
193. Kentish Times 1925
194. Heads of Royal Artillery 1860 –1914 Volume 3 - Major General Sir John Headlam - Royal Artillery Institution
195. Kentish Times – March 8th 1929
196. Firepower – The Royal Artillery Museum, The Royal Arsenal Woolwich
197. Jessica Vale – Museum Collections Manager, Bexley Museum
198. Kentish Times – March 8th 1929
199. Kentish Times – March 8th 1929
200. Finance Act Survey – Bexley 1912
201. Finance Act Survey – Bexley 1912
202. Kentish Times – March 8th 1929
203. Kentish Times – March 8th 1929
204. 'Old spoon could hold the key' News Shopper – Roger Wright – July 19th 2000
205. National Census of England and Wales 1881
206. 'Bexley Mosaic' Workers Educational Association Chapter 2 – Ed Joy Saynor M.A. 1977
207. Jessica Vale – Museum Collections Manager, Bexley Museum
208. Kentish Times 28th June 1929 and Records of D.C. Bowyer and Sons Ltd. BU/DCB/1/3/71 – Bexley Local Studies Centre
209. Kentish Times 14th June 1929 and Records of D.C. Bowyer and Sons Ltd. BU/DCB/1/3/72 – Bexley Local Studies Centre
210. The Record - News and Notes of the Month, July 1929
211. Records of D.C. Bowyer and Sons Ltd. BU/DCB/1/3/73 – Bexley Local Studies Centre

Index

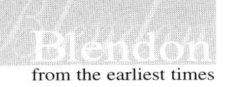

Aerial photo of development	130
Anthony, Ron	129
Anthony, Roy	129
Artefacts from the Estate	134
Arundel, Thomas	16
Avenue, The	5, 107, 135
Bailiff's Cottage	88, 89, 90, 96
Baker, Mary Ann	98
Barr-Hamilton, Malcolm	50
Bath House, the	90
Beckenham, Alfred	118
Beckenham, Sophie	118
Beckenhams, The, at West Lodge 1890's	119
Beechway	6, 53, 120, 131, 138
Berkeley, Lady Mary	19
Berkeley, Sir Charles	20
Bexley Church	39
Bexley Manor	13
Bexley Museum	6
Bexley, Borough of	9
Black Bird Fields	50
Bladigdon	13
Bladindon Court	13
Bladindon Drive	133, 135
Bladindon, Henry and Eadwin of	13
Bladinton	13
Bladynton	13
Blakeben Gate	16
Blakeben Strete	16
Blakeven Gate	16
Blakeven Strete	16
Blenden Street	53
Blendon Corner	99
Blendon Cottage	91, 99
Blendon Game Larder, The	105
Blendon Hall	7, 48, 93, 106
Blendon Hall Estate	7, 9, 13, 57
Blendon Lake	136
Blendon Parade	5

Index

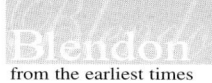

Blendon Project, The	5, 9
Blendon Road	5, 6, 10, 120
Blendon Timeline	12
Blendon Villas	87
Blunt, John	27
Bomb damage – Bladindon Drive	135
Boone, Sarah	55
Borgnis, Carl	100
Bottom Lake	8, 140
Bourne, Judith	21
Bowes Lyon, Claude	84, 140
Bowyer, D C	6, 58, 127
Bowyer, Jim	6, 7, 128
Boyd, John	47, 53
Brett, Sir Edward	19, 22
Brett/Sawbridge connection, The	24
Brewster, Edward	19
Bridgen Road	10
Bridgen School	99
British Museum, the	7
Buck, Arthur	129
Camden, William	17
Campbell Family 18th and 19th century	70
Campbell, Anna Maria	69, 72, 76
Campbell, Fanny	74
Campbell, Julia Elizabeth	72
Campbell, Julia Frances	74
Campbell, Reverend Colin Alexander	69
Campbell, William Johnson	69, 76
Castelayn, Henry	16
Castell, Rev. F de P	13
Castilayn, Simon	16
Caswall, George	23, 27
Cave, William	16
Cedar Grove	120
Champneis memorial	17
Chelmer Cottage	135
Clover Field	53
Crofton Avenue	135

Index

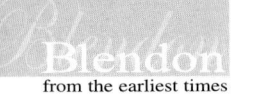

Crompton, Charles	48
Cunliffe, Sophia	93
Danson Estate	16
Danson Mansion	47
Davison, Thomas	99
Delamotte, Charles	44
Delamotte, Elizabeth	39, 40, 43, 44
Delamotte, Esther	38
Delamotte, Thomas	35
Delamotte, William	38
Desaguliers, Thomas	47
Destruction of Hall in 1934	132
Dolben, Sir William	48
Drainage Map 1898	100
Drive, The	53, 133, 138
East Lodge – top of Beechway	87
Elmwood Drive	10, 50
Eltham, royal palace of	16
Estate from Danson Road	128
Exchange Alley	25
Ferbie of St Paul's Cray-Hill	17
Fetter Lane Society	44
Fielden, John	99
Fisher, Brett	35
Fisher, Elizabeth	23
Fisher, John Brett	21, 23, 26
Franklin, Benjamin	40
Fuller, J M	96
Garrick, David	36
Gerard-Cosein, Lady Mary	19, 21
Gerrard, Sir Gilbert	19
Golden Lion Inn	66
Goldsmith, Oliver	36
Greenwich, royal palace of	16
Gudsell, James	53
Haddock, Mary	50
Haddock, Richard	48
Hall Place	6
Hall, Hazel	106

Index

Harley, Robert	27
Harper, George	98, 121, 122
Henry of Blendon	13
Hill, Francis	17
Hodgson, Henrietta Mildred	83
Hogarth, William	36
Holland, Geoff	6, 7
Holland, William	44
Horn Brass, St Mary's Church	16
Howell, Steven	98
Hoys Field	84
Humphrey Repton	62
Inner Library, The	108
James Gudsell Map of 1783	51
James, Mrs Elizabeth	46
Jay, Anna J Riggs	99, 100, 128, 140
Jay, Carl	99
Jay, Charles Augustus	95
Jay, Emma Marie Louise	104
Jay, Louis	95
Jay, Sophia Cunliffe	99
Jay, Sophie Emily	104
Jay, William Cunliffe Pickersgill	100
Jay's Cottages	5, 34, 53, 87, 88, 138
Johan de Bladigdone	14
John of Bladindon	13
Johnson, Alfred James	124
Johnson, Henry James	124
Johnson, May	106, 123
Johnson, Samuel	36
Jordan of Bladindon	16
Kentish Times, the	11
Lainsheer, Eliza	99
Lambert, Charles	76, 140
Lamorbey	21
Lamorbey Park	58
Law, John	29
Leigh, Emma	57
Lewin, Mary	69

Index

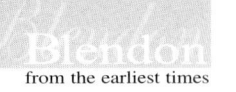

Lewin, William	69
Lidington, Harold	97
Lion Road	66
Lodge, The	6, 99
Lodge, Theodore	99
Long Meadow	53
Maberley, Evan	85
Macauley, Catherine	34
Map of Blendon 1766	49
Map of Estate 1825	71
Maps showing Blendon and Albany Park	131
Marshall, William	17
May, Nathaniel	17
McGready, Peter	122, 131
Meadow	53
Molesworth, Lord	23
Moore, Frederick	96
Moravians, the	44
Mrs Jay's Funeral Cortege in March 1929	116
Mulberry tree at the Sanctuary	22
Newton, Sir Isaac	33
North Cray Road	15
Nunn, Beverley	50
Pattison, General James	47, 52, 143
Pearne, Thomas	53
Pen River	50
Penhill Road	10, 53
Phipps Hornby, Betty and Irene	109
Phipps Hornby, Brigadier-General Edmund John	101, 102, 140
Phipps Hornby, Irene	110
Pickersgill, Anna	95, 99
Pickersgill, W C	6, 9, 93, 98
Pickersgill, William C junior	95
Pickersgill/Riggs/Jay Family – 19th & 20th century	94
Piers, Reverend Henry	38, 117
Pleasure Grounds, The	6
Print of the Hall after Repton changes	59
Print of the Hall before Repton changes	59
Public House, The	99

Index

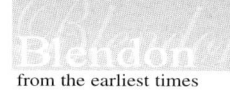

Ralph de Bladyndon	14
Rawlins, and son	17
Repton, Humphrey	58
Reynolds, Sir Joshua	36
Richmond, Nathaniel	47
Riggs, Anna	93
Riggs, George Washington	95
River Shuttle	10, 50
Robert of Bladindon	13
Rodwell, Reginald Mandeville	104
Roger of Blackwenne in Bixle	13
Roger of Bladindon	
Sanctuary, The	13, 6, 22, 53, 131
Saunders, Fred	131
Saunders, Rube	131
Saunders, William	98
Sawbridge, Jacob	23, 35, 47
Scott, Arthur	48
Scott, Lady Mary	47
Scott, William	53
Selby, Joe	133
Shaw, John	58
Sherley, Anne	17
Shrimpton, Alfred	104
Skaters on the Lake	11
Slingsby, Henry	19
Smith, Albert	118
Smith, Ellen	118
Smith, Frances Dora	84, 140
Smith, John	55
Smith, John C	82
Smith, Laura Charlotte	85
Smith, Oswald	82, 83
Smith, Oswald Augustus	84, 92
Smith, Rose	104, 119
Smiths the Bankers	56
Soden, Owen	98
South Sea Bill, the	30
South Sea House, London	27

Index

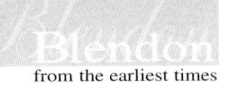

South Sea Scheme, the (Hogarth)	31
South Sea Trading Company	27
St Catherine's Chapel	66
St James the Great	7
St Mary's Church	13, 16, 50
St Mary's Church Restoration Committee	97
St Michael's Church	14
Staff at Blendon 1900	118
Steele, William	21
Stephens, Robert	53
Subsidy Rolls, the	14
Sweet Chestnut Tree in Beechway	22
Swift, Jonathan	23
Sword Blade Company, the	25
Sycamore Walk	53
Tanyard Farm	98
Tanyard Lane	10, 50
Taylor, Robert	47
Tennent, Gilbert	45
The Hall covered with ampelopsis	141
The Hall from the west	141, 142
Three Black Birds, The	5, 10, 53, 99
Timber framed house at Singleton	15
Tithe Commutation Act of 1836	84
Top Lake	139
Tucker, Elizabeth	55
Turner, Elias	23
Vale, Thomas	53
Vansittart Estate	127
Vincent, Anna Maria	69
Vincent, Dame Mary	69
Warrior the horse	113, 129
Watkins, William	98
Weald & Downland Museum	15
Wesley, Charles	35, 117
Wesley, John	35, 36
West Lodge	138
Whitaker, Sophia	95
Whitefield, George	35, 41, 42, 43, 45, 46

Index

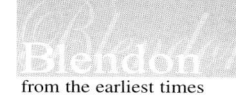

Wilkes, John	34
Woolwich and District Antiquarian Society	14
Wroth Family Tree and Crest	18
Wroth, John	17, 21
Wroth, Peter	17
Wroth, Thomas	17
Wynterfloed, John	16